THE TOTALLY AWESOME WORLD OF

LEARN ALL THERE IS TO KNOW ABOUT THE WORLD'S BIGGEST YOUTUBER

—

NEAL E. FISCHER

becker&mayer! kids

CONTENTS

FLASHBACK:
A $4 MILLION VIDEO

—

Energy and excitement were in the air. The tension was high. At the end of a long day, one lucky person (out of 456) would be nearly half-a-million dollars richer—a life-changing amount of money. Behind the scenes, nerves, anxiety, and stress coursed through the veins of Jimmy Donaldson—better known to millions as MrBeast—as he embarked on the biggest video of his life. This project was a far cry from counting to 100,000, goofing around with his friends, or talking about video games from the comfort of his bedroom. It was an ambitious undertaking in recreating *Squid Game*, one of the world's most popular TV shows!

Not only was MrBeast recreating *Squid Game*, but he was doing so in only 45 days and releasing it a mere two months after the original had first aired. To achieve this monumental task, MrBeast put in more money, more effort, and more time than he'd ever spent on a video before, with a budget of $4.2 million!

⚡ ～ SQUID GAME ～ ⚡

is a South Korean survival drama television series created by Hwang Dong-hyuk that premiered on Netflix on September 17, 2021. The show follows 456 money-hungry contestants who take part in a deadly competition for a massive cash prize. Quickly becoming a global phenomenon and pop culture sensation, *Squid Game* shattered records by becoming Netflix's most watched series at launch with 111 million viewers. The show's success continued with a second season in 2024, and a third season in 2025.

He employed over 150 people to bring it to life. And he used every available inch of studio space he had, even building sets in places like churches and a rodeo stadium. And for the first time ever, he used CGI (computer-generated imagery) to digitally extend sets (giving them a larger-than-life appearance) and to give his video the same production value as its inspiration. To help achieve these stunning visual effects, the team used Unreal Engine: the world's most advanced real-time 3D creation software, primarily used to make the world's best-selling video games.

But along with the computer effects, in true MrBeast fashion, the team used practical (or real) effects as much as possible while making the video. These included the squibs—the small explosion/gunshot effects—that every competitor wore. The squibs were controlled by an app specially created for the occasion.

Video Games Made with Unreal Engine

- **Gears of War 4**
- **Cyberpunk 2077**
- **Star Wars Jedi: Fallen Order**
- **Fortnite**
- **Batman: Arkham Knight**

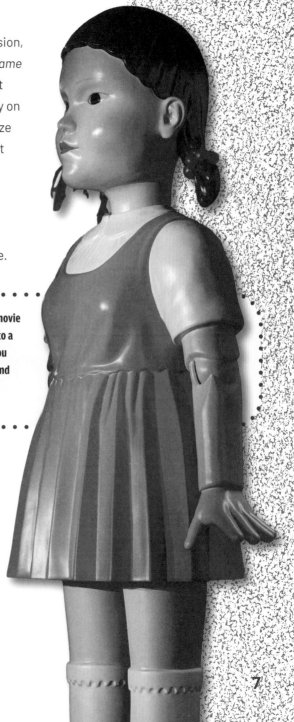

The tireless efforts of hundreds of crew members, 456 contestants, and MrBeast's vision, resulted in the final video, "$456,000 *Squid Game* In Real Life!" When the video was uploaded, it set a record for the most views in a single day on YouTube. This video wasn't just about the prize money or creating a spectacle for MrBeast—it was about pushing boundaries of what was possible on YouTube. It was about creating content that rivaled big-budget Hollywood productions on a smaller scale and bringing people together through a shared experience.

IF YOU COULD turn any Hollywood movie or television show into a realistic game that you played with friends and family, what would it be and why?

MrBeast's *Squid Game* was a visual experience that made him YouTube's biggest star and a global phenomenon. But MrBeast didn't achieve worldwide success overnight. It took hours, days, months, and years of preparation that all started in the Midwest of the United States, 23 years earlier . . .

CHAPTER

BIRTH OF
THE BEAST

JUST A MIDWESTERN
BOY

The year 1998 was like any other. The 18th Winter Olympics (XVIII) took place in Nagano, Japan; Michael Jordan's Chicago Bulls won their 6th NBA Championship and 2nd three-peat; the New York Yankees won their 24th (of 27) World Series Championship; and Google, the most powerful search engine on Earth was created and has since become its own verb. Don't believe us? Google it! Despite famous figures like French football star Kylian Mbappé, recording artist Shawn Mendes, and actress Elle Fanning being born this year, the internet would forever be changed when the future most viewed person on Earth (and perhaps in the galaxy) was born during the 5th month of the year.

James Stephen "Jimmy" Donaldson was born on May 7, 1998, in Wichita, Kansas. To his friends, family, and followers, he is just Jimmy, but just a few years down the road, he would be known the world over by another name: MrBeast. Jimmy was born to Sue Parisher, a dedicated lieutenant colonel who served honorably in the US Army for 21 years and Stephen Donaldson, also in the military. Along with his older brother, CJ, Jimmy's early years were made up of frequent movement and travel due to his parents' military careers.

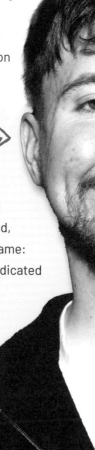

NORTH CAROLINA

1. Became a state on November 21, 1789.

2. Home to the first successful powered airplane flight (by Orville and Wilbur Wright), which took place on December 18, 1903, in Kitty Hawk.

3. Birthplace of notable inventions such as Pepsi-Cola; Vicks VapoRub; the Universal Product Code (UPC), the barcode found on most products in a store; and Krispy Kreme Donuts.

4. Home to the Biltmore Estate, the largest private residence in the United States. Nestled on 8,000 acres (3,227 ha) of land (that's 6,050 football fields), George Vanderbilt's Gilded Age mansion has 250 rooms, 35 bedrooms, 43 bathrooms, and 65 fireplaces.

5. Some of the best basketball players in the world were born in or raised here! These stars include Steph Curry; Chris Paul; Zion Williamson; Bob McAdoo; James Worthy; and Michael Jordan, the greatest basketball player of all time (and graduate of University of North Carolina), who was born in Brooklyn, New York, but grew up and learned how to dunk while sticking his tongue out in Wilmington.

The constant relocations made it difficult for Jimmy to form any long-lasting friendships. He would often feel like an outsider, struggling to connect with his peers and unable to find things in common to talk about with them. The family lived in various cities and even spent time overseas in Germany before finally settling in Greenville, North Carolina.

LOST IN
LEGO BRICKS

Before he became obsessed with YouTube (changing his life forever), Jimmy was all about LEGO. Growing up, Jimmy immediately exhibited signs of a hyper-obsessive personality. He would lose himself for hours in the world of LEGO, creating intricate structures and elaborate forts that would fill his room with colorful plastic. Having an obsessive personality means that you get fully consumed by your interest in any given subject. If it's a new song, you might listen to it on repeat for days or even weeks until you know every note, lyric, and the entire story behind the song. Perhaps it's the art of painting, where you continually paint and learn how to get better until you've mastered every element of the process. Whether it's for one week, one month, or years on end, your whole world becomes about your new obsession. The simple act of building something from nothing

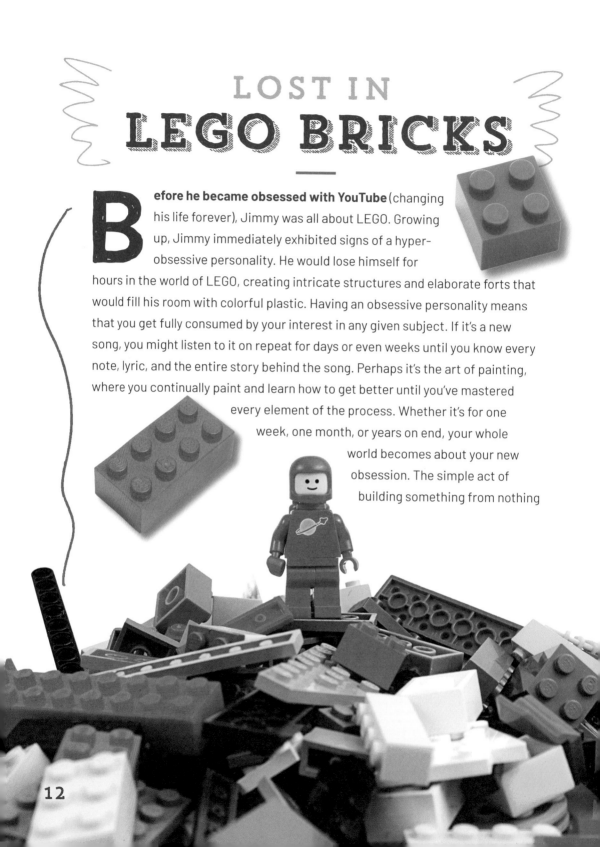

showcased Jimmy's ability to focus intensely on a project to create an eye-catching display that he could show off to the world. These early creations no doubt helped Jimmy realize he loved being a showman. This would come in handy for his future videos giving away massive prizes and building gigantic sets and obstacles for his biggest challenges.

WANT TO

be a LEGO designer? Fans can submit model designs and ideas to ideas.lego.com/projects/create. If the design reaches 10,000 votes, it has a chance to be made official. Start brainstorming now!

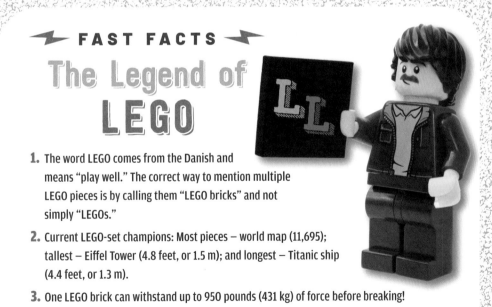

⚡ FAST FACTS ⚡
The Legend of LEGO

1. The word LEGO comes from the Danish and means "play well." The correct way to mention multiple LEGO pieces is by calling them "LEGO bricks" and not simply "LEGOs."

2. Current LEGO-set champions: Most pieces — world map (11,695); tallest — Eiffel Tower (4.8 feet, or 1.5 m); and longest — Titanic ship (4.4 feet, or 1.3 m).

3. One LEGO brick can withstand up to 950 pounds (431 kg) of force before breaking!

4. There are 915,103,765 different ways to combine six standard (2 x 4) LEGO bricks!

UNLOCKING THE POWER OF
YOUTUBE

During the early years of Jimmy's upbringing, however, life at home wasn't perfect. His mother and father separated after several years of hardship. This was painful for Jimmy and his brother. After the separation, they were raised by their mother, Sue, who worked tirelessly to provide a safe and loving environment. To take care of Jimmy and CJ as a single mother, Sue worked long hours leaving Jimmy alone with his thoughts at home. Already struggling to connect with friends, Jimmy was also struggling at school. He just wasn't interested in what he was learning and didn't connect with lessons being read directly from a book. He wanted to be more hands-on with

The Origin of YouTube

It all started with elephants. Back in February 2005, three friends came up with a brilliant idea that would change history. Chad Hurley, Steve Chen, and Jawed Karim wanted to make it easy for people to share videos online. Thus, YouTube was born. And it wasn't created in a big skyscraper or massive office with a team of thousands. The innovative trio worked out of Chad Hurley's garage. Yes, a garage. Did you know some of the most famous companies and brands in history were started in a garage? Apple, Microsoft, Google, Amazon, and even Disney! In November 2006, Google saw how popular YouTube was becoming and decided to buy it for $1.65 billion.

his learning. Some kids excel easily in school, while for others, it's a challenge. Everyone's brain works a little differently. But during these difficult times, Jimmy discovered an unexpected source of solace: YouTube.

Within the digital walls of that website, Jimmy was able to find knowledge, entertainment, community, and something he knew he could be passionate about. Just like he did with his LEGO creations, Jimmy became hyper-obsessed with YouTube. It became a safe space, offering a world of endless creativity and potential where he could escape the complexities and hardships of his daily life. He could play his favorite video games at home and then log on and see other people with similar interests playing the same games. Early on he looked up to YouTubers like Felix Kjellberg, better known as PewDiePie, and Matthew Woodworth, known as WoodysGamertag. Both creators were known for playing games online and had funny personalities. What intrigued Jimmy the most was the fact that they were able to quit their jobs and do YouTube full-time—something that Jimmy couldn't even imagine. This was possible?

No. 1 The first video ever uploaded to YouTube was by YouTube cocreator Jawed Karim and was recorded on Karim's camera by his friend Yakov Lapitsky. It was called "Me at the Zoo" and is just 18 seconds long. In the video, Jawed is visiting the San Diego Zoo, talking about—you guessed it—elephants. You can still watch the video today where it has amassed over 320 million views. After the video was uploaded, YouTube grew super fast. People loved that they didn't need to be a computer scientist to upload their videos or watch other videos from around the world.

BECOMING
THE BEAST

Once **Jimmy heard** about the success of others on YouTube, he decided to give it a try. At the ripe old age of 11, Jimmy uploaded his first video: gameplay from *Battle Pirates*. When his video went online, it immediately got 20,000 views! From that moment on, Jimmy was hooked. Unfortunately, after some friends at school learned about his channel, he became self-conscious about his videos and deleted all his content. But Jimmy eventually came back because he couldn't shake the feeling that he was destined to be a professional YouTuber. In February 2012, at age 13, Jimmy uploaded his first video under his new name, MrBeast6000. Why did Jimmy pick that name? It's mostly random. When you start an account on Xbox, if you don't choose your own gamertag (or username), the system auto generates one for you. Jimmy's Xbox chose MrBeast6000, and the rest is history.

XBOX

1. The first Xbox console was released on November 15, 2001, for $299 by Microsoft and competed with the Sony PlayStation 2, Nintendo GameCube, and Sega Dreamcast.

2. There have been four generations of Xbox (Xbox, Xbox 360, Xbox One, and Xbox Series S/X) with nine total consoles released since 2001.

3. The Xbox Network (formerly known as Xbox Live), where users can play games together online, launched in 2002 and currently has over 200 million monthly users.

4. The controller (known for its bulky size) that shipped with first-generation systems was nicknamed "Duke" after the son of Brett Schnepf, a founding member of the hardware team who worked on the controller.

5. According to "Father of the Xbox," Seamus Blackley, the reason Xbox uses the color green in branding is simply due to designer Horace Luke only having a green marker on him when he started drawing up designs.

IF YOU

could choose your own Xbox gamertag, what would it be? If you already have one, why did you choose that name? Xbox allows twelve characters including spaces. Example: TOtaLyAwsOme

__ __ __ __ __ __ __ __ __ __ __ __
1   2   3   4   5   6   7   8   9   10   11   12

The more he recorded videos, the more Jimmy became obsessed with YouTube and all it had to offer. He was intrigued by how someone could build a career on YouTube. Many YouTubers like PewDiePie put themselves front and center on their channels, but Jimmy decided to remain off camera, so he wouldn't have to show his face, which was riddled with acne. His first goal was to try and master the YouTube algorithm so that his videos would become popular and go viral. His first videos focused on gaming with favorites such as *Minecraft* and *Call of Duty: Black Ops II*, in a style known as "Let's Play." He would have the game footage on-screen and give commentary over it. Some videos had him giving tips about the game, estimating the wealth of other YouTubers, or commenting on YouTuber drama. He started to see success when he began making videos poking fun at the "worst intros" to different YouTubers. As he was learning more about YouTube and how to get his videos in front of more eyeballs, Jimmy learned that PewDiePie, at that time, was getting 7.5 million views per day, which meant he was getting paid $13,000 a day. Wow! PewDiePie would go on to become the most followed YouTuber in the world for nine consecutive years.

That is, until a young kid from Greenville, North Carolina, kicked him off the top spot.

THANKS TO

YouTube's Creator program, YouTubers can make money with advertisements placed during a video. You must have 1,000 subscribers with 4,000 valid public watch hours to be able to participate.

The Top Ten
MOST VIEWED
YouTube Videos of All Time!
(As of January 2025)

1. **Baby Shark Dance** by Pinkfong

2. Despacito by Luis Fonsi ft. Daddy Yankee

3. **Wheels on the Bus** by Cocomelon

4. Johny Johny Yes Papa by LooLoo Kids

5. Bath Song by Cocomelon

6. **See You Again** by Wiz Khalifa ft. Charlie Puth

7. Shape of You by Ed Sheeran

8. Phonics Song with Two Words by ChuChu TV

9. Uptown Funk by Mark Ronson ft. Bruno Mars

10. Gangnam Style by PSY*

*Gangnam Style by PSY was the first video to ever reach 1 billion views.

WHAT ABOUT BASEBALL?

While Jimmy experimented and fell in love with YouTube, he still didn't have many friends. He didn't enjoy school and admits he hardly ever brought his books home. His goal was to become a full-time YouTuber. The only problem? His mother, Sue, had no idea. She assumed all the talking and yelling from his room was Jimmy playing with his friends. Early on in his career, Jimmy's views and subscribers weren't exactly what he had hoped for, which was disappointing to someone who was so determined at a young age. So, he took a liking to baseball. Much like LEGO and YouTube, he became obsessed practicing nearly two to three hours a day and becoming good enough to consider playing in college one day.

PLAY BALL

During his time at Greenville Christian Academy, Jimmy played varsity baseball for the Knights and racked up these impressive stats: 70 GP (Games Played), 0.424 Batting Average, 511 OBP (On Base Percentage), 81 Hits, and 65 RBI (Runs Batted In).

Despite being on a team, he struggled with team-bonding activities and carrying on conversations with teammates and coaches (unless it was about YouTube). But Jimmy loved the game and kept playing. Unfortunately, at the age of 15, he was diagnosed with Crohn's disease, and it would be the biggest sign that perhaps he had already found his calling.

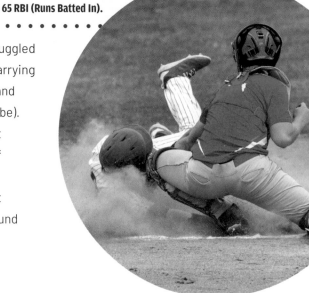

Jimmy described the pain of Crohn's like a knife sliding across the inside of his stomach. His days were practically ruined by having to go to the bathroom 20 times a day. During baseball practice or games, he'd be throwing up behind the dugout. It made school impossible. It made baseball impossible. And life was just hard. Jimmy lost between 40 and 60 pounds (18 and 27 kg) and felt like he was skin and bones with a face full of acne. All he wanted to do was lie in bed and not get up. He felt like he had no one to talk to and that his chronic condition was taking over his life.

It was a time filled with uncertainty, Jimmy wasn't sure what he could do with himself during the day. He was mostly holed up in his room. The light of the computer screen, though, invited him into a new world where things didn't seem as hard.

What Is CROHN'S DISEASE?

Crohn's disease is a lifelong autoimmune condition that affects the digestive system, which helps you break down food and get nutrients. It can cause symptoms like belly pain, diarrhea, weight loss, tiredness, bleeding, and fever. Doctors don't know what causes the disease but think it may be related to an autoimmune reaction—this means your body's immune system (which is supposed to protect you) mistakenly attacks healthy cells.

While there's no cure for Crohn's, medications, special diets, and sometimes surgery can help. As with many chronic conditions (meaning it doesn't go away completely), someone might feel fine one moment but be in a lot of pain when symptoms strike. With the right treatment, many people with Crohn's can live a healthy life.

THE TASTE OF
SUCCESS

Jimmy may not have had a steady friend group, and his mom might have been working a lot, but he did realize he truly loved YouTube. He decided to give up baseball and went full force into creating content. He would study for hours and hours every day on how to get likes, views, and subscribers; the best microphones and cameras; tips on lighting and editing; what software to use; and so on. The talking heads on YouTube became his new teachers, and after hours of mentally downloading information, Jimmy taught himself all the skills he needed to succeed. While he may have struggled in the rigid structure of a typical school environment, Jimmy thrived on the internet and was going full speed ahead. As he kept grinding, he always told himself that he'd tell his mom about his new obsession once he hit 10,000 subscribers. But something else happened that let Jimmy know he was on the right track . . . he started making money.

Jimmy started small, making $1 a day, and when he hit 75,000 views, he made his first $100 off YouTube. Instead of buying pizza or a new video game, Jimmy invested his earnings back into his channel to continually grow, evolve, and make his content better—a practice he follows to this day. Every dime he makes (that doesn't go to a charity or person in need) is reinvested to make the next video bigger and better. With his new earnings, Jimmy was able to save up and buy a good microphone and a new computer. After he got the new equipment, his videos changed in a big way: Jimmy was starring in them.

 # YouTube

Did you know there are around 800 million videos on YouTube, with some estimates reaching as high as 1 billion? Every minute, 500 hours of new video content is uploaded to the site. That's 30,000 hours of video every hour, and over 720,000 hours every single day! If you attempted your own MrBeast-like challenge—"I Watched Every YouTube Video Uploaded in One Day!"—it would take you (drumroll, please) 82 years to finish them all. That's just videos uploaded to the site in one day. Unless you're a vampire (and therefore immortal), it's probably not the most realistic challenge.

But if you ARE a vampire (whether you sparkle or not) and decided to watch every single video on YouTube if they stopped uploading today, it would take you 156 million hours. That's 17,810 years of nonstop watching. Talk about too much screen time!

Jimmy was now front and center, talking to the camera and letting his personality shine—something his growing legion of followers enjoyed. He may have had trouble socializing, but that little camera lens didn't judge him or make fun of him, and it felt like people were just listening. By introducing IRL (In Real Life) content on his feed, showing his offline personality online (and humanizing him more), Jimmy's audience began to grow. Now Jimmy was on his way to finally figuring out how YouTube really worked. But he did have one obstacle in front of him.

After Jimmy graduated from Greenville Christian Academy in 2016, his mother, Sue, told him that he had to go to college. She grew up in a generation when after you graduated from high school, you went to college. College is very important for some jobs, like lawyers and doctors, while for some people, college can be a great experience but isn't mandatory. Sue told Jimmy that if he wanted to live in her house rent-free, he had to go to college. College was the last place Jimmy wanted to be because he was focused on his YouTube career, but he wasn't making enough money to go full-time on YouTube to support himself. So, when given the choice of college and having a roof over his head, or no college and nowhere to live, Jimmy chose to give college a try. But what he didn't know was that he was a lot closer to going viral than he thought—it would just take a few weeks and a few crazy YouTube stunts to change the course of his life forever.

THE ULTIMATE YOUTUBER STARTER KIT

So, you want to be a YouTuber? Or maybe you just want to make funny videos by yourself or with friends? Everyone needs to start somewhere! Thanks to modern technology being so accessible, it's never been easier to become a content creator. Sprinkle in some creativity, determination, and hard work (and this arsenal of tools and suggestions), and you'll be well equipped to embark on an epic journey of content creation.

CAMERA: You're just starting out. You don't need a $1,000 camera! You have a complete movie studio in your pocket with your phone. Use your cellphone or borrow your parents'. If you'd like to step up your game, check out a Sony ZV-1F: the perfect point-and-shoot camera for vloggers.

MICROPHONE: No matter how nice your videos look, if your sound stinks, no one will enjoy them. We want to hear you! Use an external microphone that plugs into your phone, computer, or camera. For wireless capabilities, check out the Rode Wireless Pro or DJI Wireless microphones.

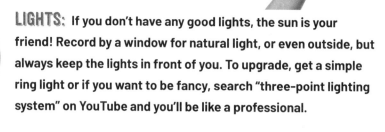

LIGHTS: If you don't have any good lights, the sun is your friend! Record by a window for natural light, or even outside, but always keep the lights in front of you. To upgrade, get a simple ring light or if you want to be fancy, search "three-point lighting system" on YouTube and you'll be like a professional.

TRIPOD: Videos that aren't shaky are the best kind of videos. Check out tripods for your cellphone or camera so you know your videos will be stabilized. A tripod is great if you record by yourself. Better yet? Ask a friend to help you record.

COMPUTER: Get access to a computer to help you edit and upload your videos. Don't have your own just yet? Ask your parents or a friend, or check if your school or local library has one you can use.

EDITING: There are tons of free and paid editing programs for all levels of experience. Want to edit on your phone? Try CapCut. Have an Apple? It comes with iMovie. Want to use some more professional software? Check out DaVinci Resolve, Adobe Premiere, or Final Cut Pro.

EDUCATION: Never stop learning! Whether you're 9 or 90, try and learn one new fact or skill every day. How did Jimmy become MrBeast? By watching YouTube videos and learning how to make them. The best place to learn how to shoot, light, edit, publish, and make videos is, of course, YouTube!

THINK BEFORE YOU POST!

Remember, it's important to think about what you publish online. Once you post or publish your content, it exists forever. Ask yourself: In one hour, or one week, or one year from now, do I want this content out in the world?

How to Speak YouTube:
A GLOSSARY

· ·

Exploring YouTube is like following a secret treasure map. There are twists and turns, and instead of gold (where X marks the spot), you get endless hours of content that can make you laugh, cry, or learn something new. Like a treasure map (with its coded messages and puzzles), YouTube has its own language, filled with words that might seem confusing. To help you become a pro at YouTube, here are a few key terms and their definitions to help you get started on your own journey.

Abbreviations & Acronyms: Condensed words or phrases that describe or represent something. YouTube examples are: IRL (In Real Life), SEO (Search Engine Optimization), GRWM (Get Ready With Me), or AMA (Ask Me Anything).

Algorithm: A program that watches your habits on a social media app and decides what to show you or recommend. The more you search something, the more you'll see!

Analytics: A set of data (facts or statistics) that can show YouTubers things like how many people watched a video, how long they watched it, and what location they were in when they watched it.

Avatar: A picture or logo that represents you or your channel on YouTube—it has nothing to do with the movie with the blue people. MrBeast's first avatar was a tiger.

Clickbait: A video that often uses misleading or sensational headlines, descriptions, or thumbnails in an effort to get the most clicks and views. Example: "You Won't Believe What MrBeast Said!"

Collab: When two YouTubers collaborate on a video(s) to help introduce new viewers to their content. Former NASA engineer and YouTuber Mark Rober has collab'd with MrBeast several times.

Influencer: A creator (with a sizeable following) who collaborates with brands to promote or sell products. MrBeast promotes his chocolate and burgers but also inspires giving back to the community!

Monetization: How does MrBeast keep making cool videos? By making money on them. Monetization is the way YouTubers make their money, usually through ads placed in their videos.

Retention: A type of stat showing how long viewers watch a video before clicking on something else. It helps creators see how well their video is being received. It's MrBeast's favorite data to study. Keep 'em hooked!

Subscriber: Someone who likes your content enough to follow and be alerted when a new video or piece of content drops. Along with views, the number of subscribers one has is the most important YouTube metric.

Tag: No, we're not talking about the game you play on the playground. These are keywords you include with your video to help it show up when people are searching for those same keywords on YouTube. Tags are usually indicated with a "#" symbol just before the keyword, as follows: #MrBeast.

Thumbnail: A small picture (think book cover) that represents a video enticing people to click. MrBeast is an expert with thumbnails, often photoshopping his image in crazy ways to maximize viewership.

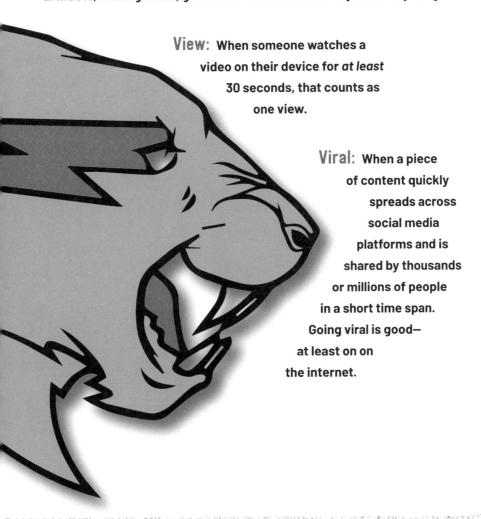

Unboxing: A popular type of video where a YouTuber opens packages of various types of things: new computer equipment, toys, priceless artifacts, trading cards, gifts from subscribers. Pretty much anything!

View: When someone watches a video on their device for *at least* 30 seconds, that counts as one view.

Viral: When a piece of content quickly spreads across social media platforms and is shared by thousands or millions of people in a short time span. Going viral is good— at least on on the internet.

CHAPTER

GOING
VIRAL

CRACKING THE
CODE

MrBeast had some minor success once he moved himself in front of the camera and let the world see the face behind the Beast. At first, he thought that his channel would be lucky to get 3,000 subscribers. But once he hit that number, and it kept growing, MrBeast thought he could be onto something and made sure to keep grinding. It took him a year and a half to get his first 1,000 subscribers. It took almost a year to get to 2,000 subscribers. Then he got 1,000 more subscribers in 11 days! Progress! After that, to go from 4,000 to 5,000 subscribers, it only took 12 days. Things were picking up and they were picking up fast. It took him 3 years to hit 5,000 subscribers, and when he hit that number, something special happened. His mom started to watch all

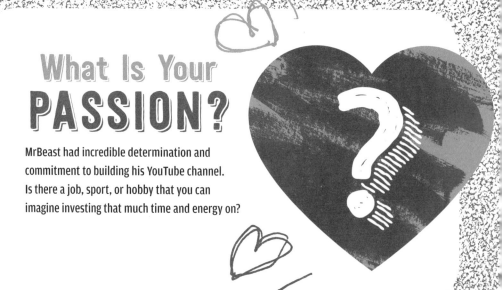

What Is Your
PASSION?

MrBeast had incredible determination and commitment to building his YouTube channel. Is there a job, sport, or hobby that you can imagine investing that much time and energy on?

his videos. Sure, he might have been a little embarrassed. We all get embarrassed sometimes if a parent watches us perform or do something that we've been practicing. But this signaled a turning point for MrBeast because now his mother knew what he was doing and was taking notice. This is what he wanted as a career, and she had a front-row seat to the greatest rise of a content creator ever! At the 5,000-subscriber mark, he gave advice to all of his fans: "Be original. Have fun." That seems like good advice for anyone, even if they aren't a YouTuber.

It's hard to even imagine a world where MrBeast doesn't have millions of subscribers, but in order to hit his first 10,000 subscribers, it took MrBeast 450 videos! Back at home, after his mother gave him the ultimatum about college, MrBeast reluctantly agreed to enroll at East Carolina University, a public university in Greenville. At first, MrBeast kept trying to tell his mother that he didn't want to be at school, he didn't want to go to class, and he even asked her to do his homework for him. Sue was adamant that he had to go to class because she cared about him and wanted what was best for him. He didn't have the best grades, and she wanted him to commit to school.

What she didn't know was how committed MrBeast was to YouTube. MrBeast's heart just wasn't in college. All he dreamed about day and night was making YouTube videos. But he wasn't making enough money to move out. He had no job. And to everyone on the outside, it looked unrealistic that he could make a career out of being a content creator. So MrBeast became depressed. After two weeks of attending college, he just stopped going. Full stop. He didn't even tell his mom. Instead, he sat in his car all day working on videos, editing, or writing scripts. Then, he would come home and pretend like he had been at class all day. Definitely not recommended when you're paying for school!

COLLEGE

You've probably seen college football games on TV or people walking around with hoodies that say UCLA or Harvard, or fraternity or sorority names in Greek letters, like $\Gamma\Phi B$ (Gamma Phi Beta) or $\Sigma A E$ (Sigma Alpha Epsilon). These are college students who applied (with grades, essays, and extracurriculars from high school) and were accepted into these institutions. College is a place where people can choose to go and learn more about a particular subject after they finish high school. It can be something they want to continue learning, like music, theater, math, science, or perhaps a brand-new subject or skill to help them figure out their career. Colleges offer classes in almost every subject you can think of—even **Taylor Swift**. Several colleges in the United States have Taylor Swift-themed classes; for example, Stanford University has a class called "Taylor Swift's All Too Well (10 Week Version)," which is an in-depth analysis of her lyrics.

BREAKING
OUT

**M**rBeast's growth started to get real.** He started earning $20,000 a month in ad revenue. He finally was making money! A good amount of money. He worked up the courage to tell his mom that he was failing school and that he was moving out. At first, she wasn't happy, because she just couldn't see how this YouTube thing would work. But MrBeast only cared about taking care of his mother and started to make so much money that it amounted to her entire years' salary in just a month. In the video "Giving My Mom $100,000 (Proudest Day Of My Life)," MrBeast gives his mom enough money to pay off her house so that she never has to make another mortgage payment again. After this, Sue was able to retire. But she ended up getting the most important job she had since being MrBeast's mother. She joined his company and has been in charge of all his bank accounts to make sure all the money is managed correctly. MrBeast did what he said he was going to do: he took care of his mother, paid off her house, allowed her to retire, and gave her a spot in his company. They could all breathe a sigh of relief and never have to worry about money again. Pretty cool when you think about it.

IF YOU could give your mom or dad one special gift, no matter the cost, what would it be and why?

At 30,000 subscribers MrBeast moved out of his mom's house and officially stopped going to East Carolina University. Now that he was on his own, living in an apartment, there were no distractions. MrBeast found a group of friends and fellow content creators who could help each other succeed. Together they decided there would be no drinking, no drugs, and no dating, just obsessing about YouTube, from waking up to going to sleep. He even remembers getting up and having an 18-hour Skype call with his friends—studying trends, learning the algorithm—and then going to bed right after it. He was all in.

His early videos continued to build momentum and net him more followers, but it was a few key videos that truly catapulted him into the YouTube spotlight, changing his life forever. It all started with oddly captivating videos that contained a mind-numbing concept that went on for a long time. One of the first was "Reading The Entire *Bee Movie* Script But Everytime They Say 'Bee' I Repeat All the Previous Bees," and it was a hit. The video is simply 90 minutes of MrBeast, in front of the camera, reading the script from his phone. He would go on to record similar mind-numbing videos, like "Watching 'Dance Till You're Dead' For 10 Hours" or "Watching 'It's Everday Bro' For 10 Hours Straight." Then MrBeast finally hit big with his famous video "I Counted To 100,000!" in which he sits in a chair, wearing a Harvard T-shirt, and *literally* counts from 1 to 100,000. It was a far cry from the epic videos he releases now, but it was simple and effective, and viewers ate it up!

"I COUNTED TO 100,000"

took over 40 hours to film. MrBeast sped up the video for viewers so that the marathon counting session was condensed into a watchable video that he hoped would show off his dedication—and it did!

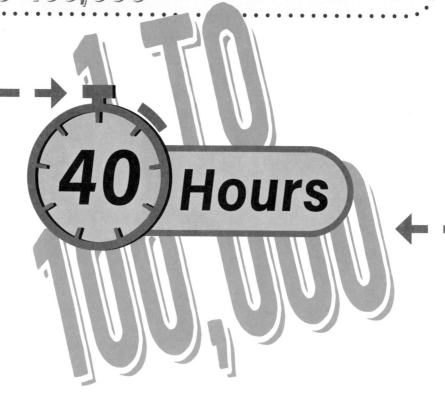

40

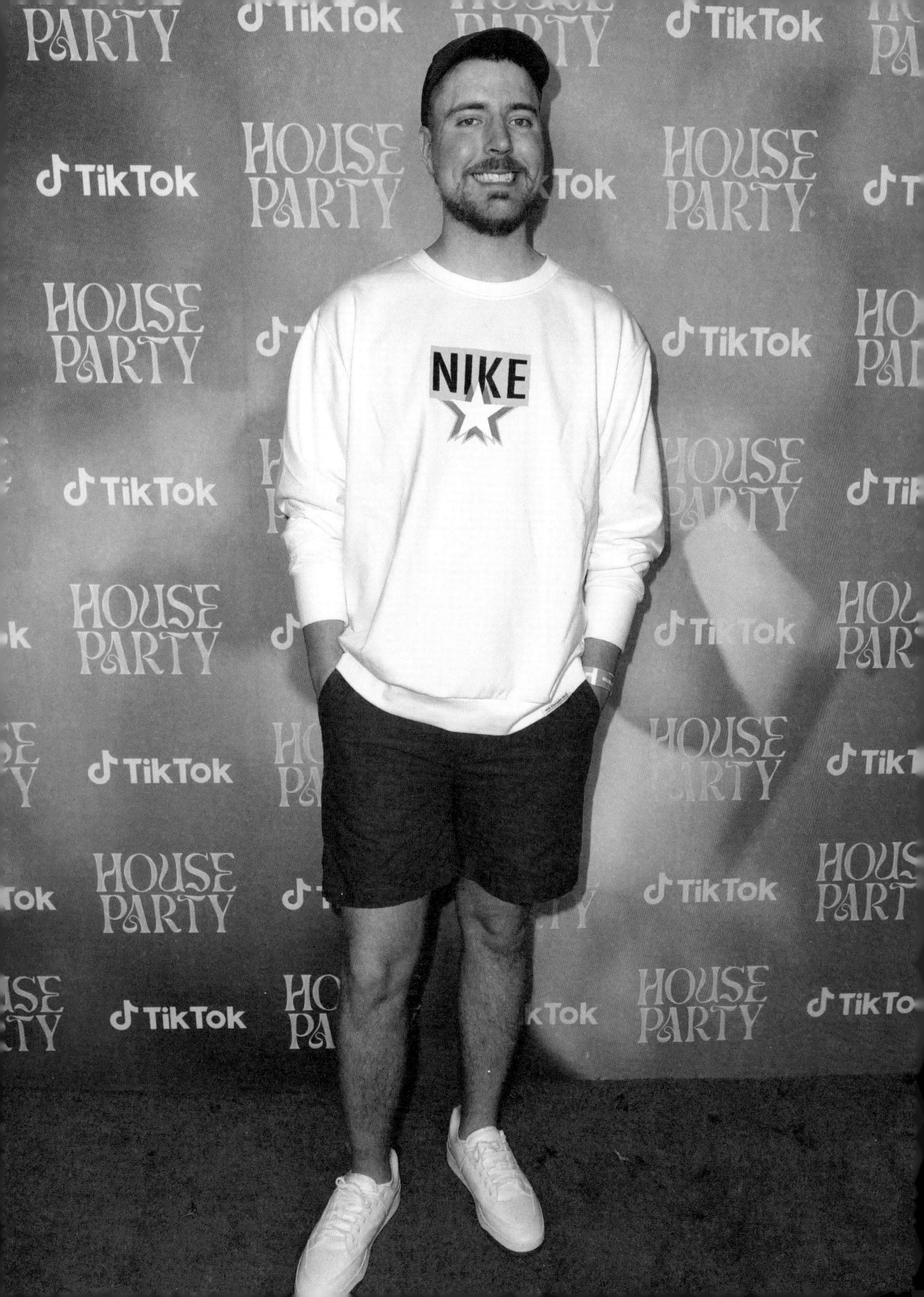
HOUSE PARTY
TikTok
NIKE

After all these fun, new videos began getting major views, one video had a major impact on him personally and brought him to a new level of success. On June 15, 2017, MrBeast uploaded "Giving A Random Homeless Man $10,000." It unlocked a new side of MrBeast and a new way of creating and watching YouTube videos. For the video, MrBeast got his first brand deal with an app called Quidd. They offered him $5,000. MrBeast said that whatever money they gave him, he was going to give to a random homeless person. MrBeast even said it should be $10,000 because it sounds better and looks better in a thumbnail. At first, the tech company didn't go for it. But Quidd ultimately agreed and gave MrBeast the money. He then did as he promised, just like he would do for every brand deal: he'd either give it away or invest it in new videos focused on helping others financially. This video showed that behind the beast, behind the camera, and behind the avatar and brand was a person with a good heart who only wanted to make the world a better place.

Viral Video
HISTORY

No one really knows what it takes to go viral. Sometimes it's just pure luck. If anyone has come close to mastering the code, it would be MrBeast. But since the dawn of YouTube and the constantly changing world of social media, it's hard to predict what will become popular. Some of the most famous "original" viral videos that are a time capsule of the early days of YouTube would surprise you. One legendary video features puppets acting out Harry Potter themes. It's called "Potter Puppet Pals: The Mysterious Ticking Noise" by @neilcic. You might be wondering *Why was this popular?* And you'd be right. That's the thing about videos that go viral. No one really knows why!

THE BEAST
GANG

Now that MrBeast was making a name for himself, he was going to need a little help. Thankfully, there were some people not too far away.

From the very beginning of MrBeast's career, it was always a priority to support and uplift his friends and family. He even refers to his team members as "family" rather than just employees. His journey may have started solo, filming and editing videos in his bedroom, but as his channel grew, he wisely realized that he needed help to keep up with the workload to be able to succeed. He slowly began adding friends or friends of friends, which became a game changer. With more people on board, quality of the videos increased, and soon after, they tackled even bigger concepts.

Stronger
TOGETHER

Have you ever partnered with a friend or group of friends on a project at school? Working in a group is a very important skill in life as most things require a team effort. That not only goes for sports, obviously, but also for all types of occupations. Even writers (like the one writing these words) can only do so much before needing a team of great people to help edit, design, and publish this book for you to read. On that note, here are famous examples of friends who went into business together and ended up having the right formula for success. Who knows? Maybe that lemonade stand or lawn-mowing service you start with your friend in the summer will turn into a million-dollar company!

1. Bill Gates and Paul Allen: Microsoft

Bill and Paul were friends in high school who loved computers. In 1975, they cofounded Microsoft. Oh, you know, that software company that seems to be on almost EVERY computer in the world that isn't an Apple.

2. Ben Cohen and Jerry Greenfield: Ben & Jerry's

Almost everyone's had at least one scoop of the delicious Ben & Jerry's ice cream, right? Friends Ben and Jerry loved ice cream so much that they opened up their first scoop shop in Vermont in 1978 by taking a $5 correspondence course at Penn State and investing $12,000.

3. Mark Zuckerberg, Dustin Moskovitz, Chris Hughes, Eduardo Saverin, and Andrew McCollum: Facebook

While friends at Harvard University, this group cofounded Facebook in 2004. First, it was a social networking site for only college students, but when it opened up to the public, it transformed the way people interacted online. Now, billions of people use Facebook around the world.

MrBeast often creates roles specifically designed for his friends' strengths, which means they can contribute to the channel's success by being good at what they do. There's an old saying that you are only as strong as your weakest link—MrBeast carefully selects positions for the people he brings on, and there are no weak links.

DREAM TEAM

Who would you ask to join you in world domination? List your most trusted and most brilliant friends and decide what role they would have in your future company.

As a boss, MrBeast knows how to take care of his employees. He provided a group of his friends with houses around the same cul-de-sac, so they could be together in a small community. This approach means that he has a strong support team. His crew works both in front and behind the camera. MrBeast feels inspired to take his content to the next level knowing that his friends have his back. Isn't it always better when that happens? Let's take a look at the current members of his "Beast Gang."

CHANDLER HALLOW

Chandler's journey toward becoming a full-time member of the Beast Gang began in a very unexpected way—he was one of MrBeast's janitors! He was initially hired to clean up after video shoots, and then everyone soon realized his potential for on-camera work. Chandler's first appearance was in "We Are Better Than Dude Perfect," and he quickly became a fan favorite due to his likable personality, comedic timing, and laid-back demeanor. He is also scared of pickles. We all have our thing, right?

You'll Relish These
PICKLE FACTS

Just in case Chandler is reading this, here are some quick-fire, fun facts about pickles!

- America was named after Amerigo Vespucci (who traveled with Christopher Columbus). What was Amerigo's job in Spain? He sold pickles. He also stacked the ships with enough pickles to help prevent scurvy!

- Americans eat around 2.5 billion pounds (1.1 billion kg) of pickles annually, which is about 9 pounds (4 kg) of pickles per person.

- **William Shakespeare** is credited with coining the term "in a pickle," which means that someone is in a bad situation. In *The Tempest*, Alonso says "How camest thou in this pickle?" See! Now you're a Shakespeare expert.

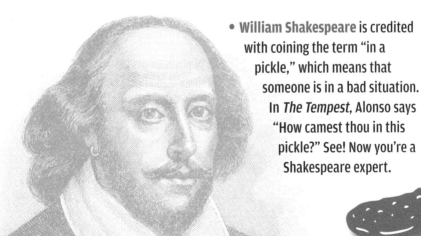

KARL JACOBS

Karl has been a fan-favorite member of the Beast Gang since 2020. He started out as an editor for MrBeast's brother, and when the team saw potential in him, he started working on MrBeast videos as a camera operator and editor. His first appearance on-screen was in the video "$60,000 Extreme Hide and Seek - Challenge"

in which he was a contestant. Having experience as an editor for MrBeast, he knew how to appear captivating and filmed himself doing things that would make the final cut. Since then, his energetic and bright personality has been a jolt of energy to the group. Karl is also a Twitch streamer (@karljacobs) and has an active YouTube channel (@Karl) with a legion of fans. His catchphrase is "What the honk?"

WHAT IS twitch?

Unlike YouTube, Twitch.tv (created in 2011) is a live-streaming platform that primarily focuses on gaming and real-time interaction between streamers and viewers, allowing creators to engage directly with the audience in the chat. Kai Cenat, one of MrBeast's frequent collaborators, is one of the site's biggest streamers.

NOLAN HANSEN

As one of the newest additions to the Beast Gang, Nolan Hansen has quickly made a name for himself. Often the butt of a joke or ribbing from the other team members, Nolan met MrBeast through YouTube, as he has his own active channel, @NolanHansen. His first

appearance in a MrBeast video was in "I Spent $1,000,000 on Lottery Tickets and WON," and he then appeared in "Last To Leave $800,000 Island Keeps It." Nolan is known for his calm demeanor and willingness to take on challenges. Nolan's mom has even made an appearance in "I Spent 7 Days Buried Alive."

TAREQ SALAMEH

Tareq was primarily known as the chief camera operator for MrBeast. While overseeing hundreds of cameras, he also became the singular voice behind the camera before also joining the gang on-screen. Originally from Palestine and raised in Saudi Arabia, Tareq is an integral part of the team. MrBeast first found Tareq at a comedy show where Tareq was doing stand-up. MrBeast saw something special in Tareq and it's been a match made in heaven ever since.

Stand-Up COMEDY

WHAT'S THE DEAL WITH ...?

Have you ever seen a stand-up comedy show? Or watched one on Netflix, YouTube, or TikTok? It's a hard gig! You have to prepare several minutes of stories and jokes, and sometimes people don't laugh or even tell you you're not funny. Do you think you could write three minutes of jokes and perform it for your friends or family? Give it a try. It's harder than you think!

CHAPTER

BUILDING THE BEAST EMPIRE

INTERNET
DOMINATION

hile MrBeast has a huge social media following on various apps, his real moneymaker is his YouTube empire. What do I mean by empire? An empire is bigger than a company and is known by a huge number of people. Empires also have power, given their success and influence. It may have started small, but like all empires, it grew bigger than anyone imagined. For MrBeast, that means his main channel (where most of his videos are posted) grew into a collection of five channels that work together—giving him nearly 500 million subscribers. Do you subscribe to all of them? Either way, here is a breakdown of all five channels— though remember, the numbers get bigger every day!

THE CHANNELS OF MRBEAST

MrBeast

@MrBeast | **Subscribers: over 360 million**

This is where it all began—@MrBeast is the home to MrBeast's most popular videos. If you could only subscribe to one channel, it should be this one. Here you'll find insane challenges, jaw-dropping stunts, cameos from other YouTubers, and heartwarming giveaways and prizes. If you want the most ambitious ideas and projects packed into a short video, look no further than this channel.

MrBeast 2

@MrBeast2 | Subscribers: **over 48 million**

This channel only has a handful of videos, but it does have MrBeast's largest collection of YouTube shorts. Many of those are on MrBeast's TikTok, but here you'll find popular shorts, such as "$10,000 Girl Scout Cookies," "I Am the World's Greatest Samurai," and "This Game Is Wild" (featuring Logan Paul and Kai Cenat).

Beast Reacts

@BeastReacts | Subscribers: **over 35 million**

On this channel, MrBeast and his friends react to viral videos or funny and interesting content—as the title suggests, they REACT! From cool inventions to crazy stunts, the page is all about sharing reactions for what's online. It's a lighter side to the empire with less frills; you get to watch the gang have fun and enjoy the internet.

Beast Philanthropy

@BeastPhilanthropy | **Subscribers: over 27 million**

This channel is entirely dedicated to giving back. It's the perfect place for MrBeast to document all his charitable efforts and partnerships with other organizations as they open food pantries, provide clean water in Africa, hold massive giveaways, or build houses and schools. Every view, ad, or brand deal from this channel directly supports these causes.

MrBeast Gaming

@MrBeastGaming | **Subscribers: over 46 million**

If you're not into watching super-long form videos yet and just like video games, this is the place to be. This channel features MrBeast and the gang playing popular games like *Fortnite*, *Among Us*, and *Minecraft*.

WHERE DOES MRBEAST ACTUALLY MAKE HIS VIDEOS?

—

When Dorothy, the Scarecrow, the Tinman, and the Cowardly Lion went off to see the Wizard, they had to travel a long way down the yellow brick road to get to the massive building that housed the great and powerful Oz. In order to see the great and powerful MrBeast, you need to go to Greenville, North Carolina, the 12th largest city in North Carolina. There you will find his sprawling complex known as Studio C, which is a 50,000 square-foot (4,645 m²) playground for creativity and jaw-dropping stunts.

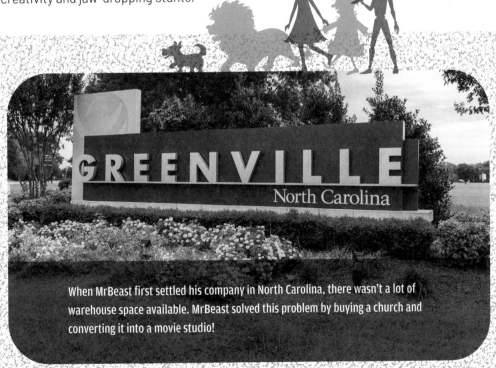

When MrBeast first settled his company in North Carolina, there wasn't a lot of warehouse space available. MrBeast solved this problem by buying a church and converting it into a movie studio!

It's not just one studio but acres of land and several buildings. In the main building, you'll find a control room packed with screens and high-tech equipment, where Jimmy and his producers can watch hundreds of cameras capture all the moments during the filming of some of the bigger videos, like "Age 1 - 100 Fight For $500,000" or "100 Kids Vs 100 Adults For $500,000." The studio itself has super-high ceilings that are soundproofed and equipped with hundreds of sprinklers for fire protection. With the building's advanced technology, MrBeast's compound is simply indestructible.

! TOTALLY AWESOME FACTS !

The Computer Chronicles

1. The term "computer bug" (a term used when something is off with your computer) comes from an actual bug! In 1947, engineers at Harvard University found a **moth** stuck in the computer that caused a malfunction. The bug was carefully removed, and the term has been used ever since to describe technical glitches!

2. The first general-purpose electronic digital computer was called **ENIAC** (Electronic Numerical Integrator and Computer) and was built in 1945. It weighed about 30 tons and took up an entire room! It was so powerful at the time that it could calculate a problem in 30 seconds that would take a person 20 hours! Talk about a time-saver!

3. Before Google, the early versions of the internet had some funny names. The first search engine ever was called Archie, a clever nickname for the word "archives" (a collection of accessible information).

Along with shooting stages, the complex includes offices for the Beast Gang, boardrooms, and other areas where all the behind-the-scenes work gets done. The walls are even covered in whiteboard paint, which allows MrBeast and his team to sketch ideas on them. In the storage warehouse, you might find an iPhone the size of a person, rubber chickens, baby dolls, and a ton of other props that have been used or will be used at some point. Inside the studio, you'll find all the Beast Reacts and Beast Gaming rooms seen on-screen. But perhaps the most important rooms are the editing suites where all his videos are edited. How can MrBeast possibly edit hundreds of hours of footage to create 15- to 20-minute videos? He does so with a staff of editors who use high-end, high-speed Apple and PC computers that are each worth around $20,000!

You might call MrBeast a workaholic as he practically *lives* at his studio. MrBeast has an apartment just a few steps from where he creates the biggest and brightest ideas for YouTube. It's a smaller space with a bed; a mini gym; a fridge stocked with mostly yogurt, water, and energy drinks; a TV; and a bathroom with a $2,000 heated toilet seat. Because why not? The room is secured with an electronic lock that only MrBeast can access via Bluetooth.

BLUETOOTH

Believe it or not, Bluetooth gets its name from a Viking king from the 10th century named Harald "Bluetooth" Gormsson. He was famous for uniting the tribes of Denmark—like how Bluetooth technology unites all of our phones, headphones, tablets, and computers. Take a close look at the Bluetooth symbol and then take a look at Harald's initials; you'll notice that when his initials are combined, it forms the symbol we see every day!

Why would you want to live at work and have no work/life balance? To MrBeast (and several famous CEOs and tech gurus), it's all about efficiency. MrBeast has admitted that he sometimes spends up to 20 days straight in the studio without leaving. By living at work, he can wake up, work out, shower, eat some food, and start filming within minutes—which is perfect for someone always chasing the next great video idea. But for others, that might not be the best way to operate. And that's okay. MrBeast takes his cues from people like Bill Gates, the cofounder of Microsoft, who once competed with his friends to see how little he could sleep while working on early projects. *Which is not recommended.* But because living at the studio works *for him*, MrBeast is okay with following in the footsteps of some of the world's most successful tech entrepreneurs and bright minds. He has happily shown interviewers that both he and Steve Jobs were on the cover of *Rolling Stone* magazine. It's very clear that MrBeast idolizes Jobs so much that he hopes to replicate his mark on the world. And if he does, that would be extraordinary.

STEVE JOBS
Visionary

Born on February 24, 1955, in San Francisco, California, Steve Jobs grew up to be one of the most influential people in the tech world and was a creative genius who changed the way we use technology. In 1976, Steve cofounded Apple in his parents' garage with his friend Steve Wozniak, where they created the first Apple computer. Steve had a clear vision: he wanted to make technology easy for everyone. That's why all Apple products are not only powerful but simple and beautiful. Anytime you use an iPhone, iPad, or iPod, you can thank Steve for helping create them and transforming the way we communicate, listen to music, and do homework! It's easy to see why MrBeast idolizes Steve Jobs so much. He dreamed big and was always thinking of new ideas.

MrBeast has been firm on staying put in his hometown of Greenville, North Carolina. Greenville is a city of around 89,000 people, and the community within has definitely felt MrBeast's presence since he's gotten bigger. Some days, luxury cars might be speeding around town (signaling a challenge or perhaps a grand-prize winner taking it for a joyride), and the local fire department often has to issue noise warnings to the community before big stunts or explosions, so residents don't think Greenville is at war! There will always be residents who aren't fans of the theatrics in their small town, but economically, MrBeast has been a huge boost to Greenville. His videos have generated hundreds of jobs, from video editors and camera operators to construction workers who build his sets. Also, you never know when MrBeast might leave a $10,000 tip at a local restaurant! Another way that MrBeast has given back to his community is through the partnership he has with **East Carolina University** to develop a training program for aspiring content creators. Want to be the best, learn from the best!

Despite becoming a global brand, MrBeast has always remained committed to Greenville. He loves the community's support and the affordability of the area (as opposed to big cities) that allow him to reinvest in his work. Not only has he bought hundreds of acres for his studio, but he's bought multiple properties to house his friends and employees. His studio, backlot, compound, content-creation army base, or whatever you want to call it, is a hub of immense creativity where the only limit is imagination.

THE EVOLUTION OF
MRBEAST'S STYLE

Who would have thought that **MrBeast** would go from sitting alone in his room practically talking to himself (with no viewers on the internet) to everyone in the world now wanting to talk to him. Well, MrBeast knew it was possible, but for the rest of us, that's an amazing achievement. So how has MrBeast changed aside from a new haircut, some facial hair, and A LOT more money to play with? When MrBeast first launched his channel, it was relatively simple and straightforward. In the early years, he wasn't even on-screen! Instead, he was commenting on gameplay or other people's videos. You don't need much production value to sit in a chair and count to 100,000 or read every word in the dictionary! While these videos were entertaining and ended up going viral, they were very low budget. It was made with basic hand-me-down equipment, no special lighting, and he didn't have much practice talking in front of the camera. He was a one-man production team: shooting, performing, editing, and releasing all his content.

HERE'S AN EXPERIMENT:

go to MrBeast's channel, click on one of his older videos and then click on his latest video that dropped. What differences do you notice in the editing, the camera work, the lighting, and the scale of everything that is happening?

As MrBeast's subscriber count began to climb higher and higher, he wisely reinvested all his earnings into his channel, which made his videos look and sound better. There was also a shift in the types of videos he started making once he went viral—more giveaways, more helping people, but also bigger sets and props and a more robust camera crew—not to mention more on-screen partners with the Beast Gang making more appearances. Fast-forward a few years and now he's got hundreds of cameras—some of them on drones—filming during competitions, giant explosions, and huge builds costing millions of dollars.

While MrBeast is entertaining and has great ideas, it wasn't just his personality that got him where he is today. He studied. He studied so hard, day and night, that he mastered the art of YouTube and its algorithm. He created content meticulously designed to maximize viewer retention— meaning he learned how to grab viewers' attention in the first 10 seconds. He does so with exciting previews of the video's most thrilling moments, so the viewer doesn't click away. MrBeast also realized that YouTube thumbnails are critical in a video's success. All of his thumbnails are colorful, bright, and attention-grabbing with big open-mouth expressions, bold text, and eye-catching pictures and graphics. Take, for example, "$10,000 Every Day You Survive In The Wilderness" and its thumbnail. It's MrBeast hanging from a tree with a **bloodthirsty bear** below him. Does MrBeast compete in the video? No. Is there a bear in the video? No. But you don't know that until you click on the video. And for that, the thumbnail has done its job. Genius!

Perhaps MrBeast's best business decision was translating ALL his videos, dubbing them in multiple languages, and making them accessible to non-English-speaking fans. It made his viewership skyrocket and made him beloved globally.

What Is DUBBING?

When a movie is dubbed, the script is translated into a different language. An actor is recorded performing the new script, and then the recording is synced with the words spoken in the original movie. Did you know that in Japan, MrBeast is dubbed by actress Junko Takeuchi who famously voices the anime character Naruto? If you heard MrBeast *en Español* and thought you heard the same Spanish-language voice as Toby McGuire's character in the *Spiderman* trilogy, you'd be right! That's Luis Daniel Ramirez. If you're going to be dubbed, might as well be dubbed by the best. If you could have anyone in the world be your voice when you spoke, who would you choose and why?

In recent years, it's been clear that MrBeast has shifted his tone and style to cater to changing viewer preferences. His early content was fast and frenetic. Now, as his viewers have aged with him and formed a connection, his videos have slowed down and focus more on storytelling. One great example is his "7 Days" series in which we follow his journey (usually with his friends or collaborators) as they deal with surviving, living in, or getting out of a situation. Some examples are "7 Days Stranded On An Island" and "I Survived 7 Days In An Abandoned City." These videos are longer (more than 20 minutes) and allow viewers to immerse themselves in the experience. This new style of video is also present in his Beast Philanthropy videos that give viewers a front-row seat to seeing people's lives change for the better.

IF YOU HAD TO

spend seven days without a phone or family or friends, where would you want to be for this week? Is there one place you know you could definitely NOT last seven days? A haunted mansion, a life raft in the middle of the ocean, inside a tent in the desert?

As MrBeast gets older, he will continue to innovate. It's what has kept him at the top of the mountain for so long. He will push boundaries as well as the limits of his creativity to constantly reinvent himself. If you're an aspiring YouTuber, MrBeast's story can offer some valuable advice on how to innovate, adapt, and succeed in a world that's always changing.

! TOTALLY AWESOME FACTS !

360,000,000
SUBSCRIBERS

The Stats of
MRBEAST

1. As of this publication, MrBeast's main channel on YouTube has surpassed 360 million subscribers, making it the most subscribed channel on YouTube. That's more people than live in the USA!

2. On June 1, 2024, MrBeast set a new personal record by gaining 2.1 million subscribers in only 24 hours!

3. In total, MrBeast has amassed over 25 billion views and counting.

4. He may have started with a webcam and a hand-me-down laptop that was basically broken, but MrBeast's videos now cost about $2.5 million to produce. Each.

5. MrBeast generates about $600 to $700 million a year (through ad revenue, brand deals, and merchandise), but the reason he is so successful is because he invests nearly all of the money back into his videos to continually make them better!

25,000,000,000
VIEWS

$700,000,000
PER YEAR

How High Can
MRBEAST GO?

· · · · · · · · · · · · · · · · ·

On MrBeast's 26th birthday, he tweeted out the number of views his YouTube videos had received each year of his life since he was 12 years old. These numbers are wild!

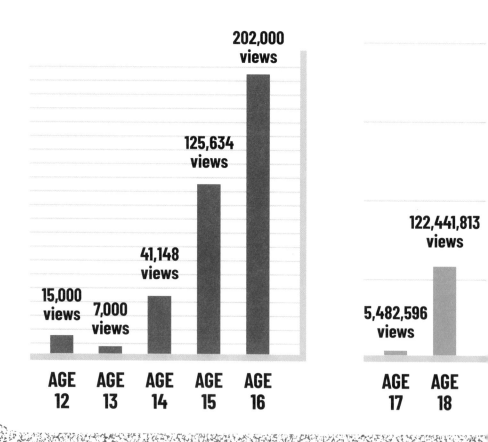

202,000
views

125,634
views

122,441,813
views

41,148
views

15,000
views

7,000
views

5,482,596
views

AGE
12

AGE
13

AGE
14

AGE
15

AGE
16

AGE
17

AGE
18

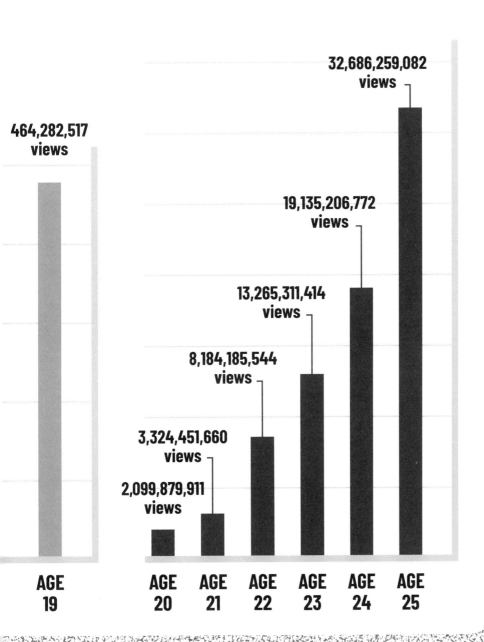

464,282,517
views

AGE
19

2,099,879,911
views

3,324,451,660
views

8,184,185,544
views

13,265,311,414
views

19,135,206,772
views

32,686,259,082
views

AGE
20

AGE
21

AGE
22

AGE
23

AGE
24

AGE
25

CHAPTER

BEAST PHILANTHROPY

FROM GAMING TO
GIVING

n a world where success is often measured by how many flashy cars you drive, how many followers you have, how big your house is, or how much jewelry or designer clothes you wear, MrBeast clearly strays from the pack with the way he lives. He's said on many occasions that he's dying with $0 in his bank account, promising to give all his money away. He refuses to live a materialistic life because all he cares about is making the best videos possible, supporting his family and friends and, most of all, helping others. MrBeast isn't interested in designer clothes (he wears his own brand most of the time), driving expensive cars like a Lamborghini (he just gives them away), or buying houses (he builds them for other people), because he chooses to live a modest life himself. While MrBeast will always be known for his wildest videos, he will forever be known as someone who believed that true wealth isn't how much you have, but how much you give.

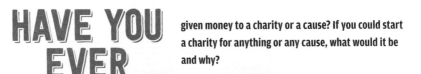

HAVE YOU EVER

given money to a charity or a cause? If you could start a charity for anything or any cause, what would it be and why?

FAVORITE CAUSES

I n **September 2020,** MrBeast launched Beast Philanthropy, a YouTube channel dedicated to charitable initiatives. Its mission is to raise funds to alleviate hunger, homelessness, and unemployment by providing life-changing grants, assistance, and both monetary and nonmonetary gifts to individuals and families. What sets Beast Philanthropy apart from other channels? All the revenue from the channel (ads, brand deals, and merch deals) goes directly to those in need. MrBeast uses the views, likes, and subscriptions of his fan base to be the change he wants to see in the world.

The first video on the Beast Philanthropy channel was titled "I Opened My Own Charity!," which introduced the world to his groundbreaking plan. In the video, he explains that he opened a food pantry in his hometown of Greenville to provide groceries to families who need them most. It wasn't just a one-time stunt for clicks or views; it was the beginning of his true purpose in life—to address hunger, homelessness, and other critical issues. Some say that he helps people because it gives him more clicks, or more ad revenue. But they are proven wrong when all that money made from those philanthropic videos goes directly to charities, food banks, worthy causes, or into the pockets of people who need some assistance.

Before Beast Philanthropy became an official channel, it was clear that MrBeast was already making waves by being generous. His early video "Giving A Random

Homeless Man $10,000" changed MrBeast's life in an instant. This video set the tone for what would become a defining aspect of his brand and his life. Whether the prize money in a video was $10,000 or $1,000,000, it was never about the money. It was about inspiring his fans to give back.

IF MrBEAST GAVE YOU

$10,000 right now, but you had to give it away, what would you do with the money? Is there a person, place, or cause you'd give it to? What are some creative ways that you could help your community?

Here are some of the highlights of how MrBeast used his influence and his channel to change the world for the better.

The Environment

MrBeast quickly realized that with all his resources, he could make an even bigger impact by teaming up with others who shared his ideals. This allowed him to tackle bigger projects like the environment. Perhaps his most famous collaboration is with his friend and former NASA engineer, YouTuber Mark Rober.

Meet Mark Rober

Mark Rober became a YouTube sensation by releasing videos and science content that make learning fun and not boring. Rober worked at NASA (National Aeronautics and Space Administration) on projects like the Mars rover *Curiosity*.

THE MARS ROVER

is a vehicle—about the size of a regular car—that drives or "roves" on the surface of Mars collecting data so that we can learn if life on Mars is even possible!

He then moved to Apple's Special Projects Group where he worked on projects dealing with virtual reality. He launched his YouTube channel in 2011, and he has more than 60 million subscribers, a number that increases daily. Rober is an advocate for autism awareness (inspired by his son who has autism) and founded Crunch Labs to create STEM (science, technology, engineering, and mathematics) learning kits for kids. With a large audience of supporters on YouTube, Rober branched out to an entirely new audience with his first TV show, *This is Mark Rober*, on Discovery GO.

#TeamTrees

In 2019, MrBeast and Mark Rober came together to launch #TeamTrees, a campaign that aimed to plant 20 million trees around the world. The project took off with MrBeast's video "Planting 20,000,000 Trees, My Biggest Project Ever!" in which followers were challenged to donate to the cause. The movement was managed by

TREES

What do you think there is more of in the galaxy—stars or trees? The answer might surprise you. According to NASA there's about 100 billion to 400 billion stars in the Milky Way galaxy. But there are more than 3 trillion trees on Earth! Considering that one large tree can provide up to a full day's oxygen to about four people, that's a lot of oxygen!

the Arbor Day Foundation, the world's largest nonprofit organization dedicated to planting trees. Soon after this launched, people from all over the world, celebrities, influencers, and companies like YouTube and Shopify chipped in ($1 per tree) to help reach the goal in just a few months. #TeamTrees, as of 2024, has raised over $24 million (meaning over 24 million trees), exceeding its original goal!

#TeamSeas

Building on the success of #TeamTrees, MrBeast and Mark Rober teamed up again in 2021 to launch #TeamSeas, an even more ambitious project aimed at removing 30 million pounds (14 million kg) of trash from the world's oceans. Just like #TeamTrees, every dollar donated removed 1 pound (454 g) of trash. The video "I Cleaned The World's Dirtiest Beach #TeamSeas" highlighted the scale of the problem and the urgent need for action. MrBeast and his team manually picked up garbage while Mark Rober, in true Rober fashion, showcased the "Interceptor": a floating trash-eating robot. Once again, the internet rallied behind the cause, and the campaign successfully met its goal, raising over $30 million to fund ocean cleanup efforts. MrBeast and Mark Rober were joined by the nonprofit organizations The Ocean Cleanup and the Ocean Conservancy to ensure that every dollar donated would have a direct impact on cleaning up our planet's waterways. These collaborations demonstrated the power of teamwork in achieving monumental goals and showcased how social media can be harnessed for good.

Operation Smile

MrBeast's philanthropy also includes efforts to help kids. In "100 Kids Smile For The First Time," Beast Philanthropy partnered with Operation Smile to provide corrective surgery for children with cleft lips and cleft palates in Puebla, Mexico. A cleft lip is when a baby is born with a gap or opening in their upper lip or cleft palate, which can make feeding and breathing more difficult.

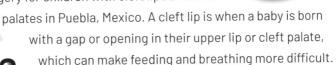

! CRAZY SCIENCE FACTS !

SEAS

The ocean covers 71% of the Earth's surface and holds about 96.5% of all Earth's water! Less than 10% of the world's ocean (and fewer than 50% of US waters) have been mapped. Because of this, the number of species that live in the ocean is unknown as they are continually discovered all the time. That means no one is quite certain if the Loch Ness Monster, Cthulhu, or the Kraken are real or not.

Since MrBeast isn't a doctor or surgeon, he partnered with a great organization to be the "boots on the ground" and work with him to help people. Operation Smile has performed over 400,000 successful surgeries in 36 countries over 40 years!

Support Exceed Worldwide

For MrBeast's video "I Helped 2000 Amputees Walk Again," he sent his team across the world (this time to Cambodia) to partner with Support Exceed Worldwide in providing prosthetics to amputees. An amputee is someone who loses a part of their body (usually an arm or a leg) because of an illness, a birth defect, or sometimes an accident. Thankfully, MrBeast and his team were able to help over 2,000 people walk again by providing services and prosthetics. A prosthetic is a special device that helps amputees by replacing a missing body part, so they can walk, run, or play sports again as well as do their normal daily activities. These appendages can be made from plastic, silicone, aluminum, and titanium.

Other ways MrBeast has helped people with healthcare are chronicled in his video "1,000 Deaf People Hear For The First Time" in which he sources $3,000,000 worth of cutting-edge hearing technology to help people hear better—or in some cases, even hear for the first time. In "1,000 Blind People See For The First Time," we learned from Dr. Levenson (the doctor who appears with MrBeast) that half of all the blindness in the world can be fixed with a 10-minute surgery. There is one big problem though: half of the world's population doesn't have access to this type of surgery or healthcare. MrBeast funded surgeries and gave access to this kind of treatment to those who needed it.

Changes around the World

MrBeast's love of giving back goes even further than the environment and healthcare. He's committed to addressing the basic needs of underserved communities around the world. One of the biggest areas of focus has been providing clean water to communities in Africa.

WATER NEEDED

Lack of clean water is one of the most pressing issues facing developing countries. It can lead to widespread health problems and disease, and it can limit opportunities for these countries to develop properly. Many people take for granted that they have clean, drinkable water right out of the tap. So, in the spirit of MrBeast, try to conserve water. By taking simple actions like turning off the tap when it's not in use, taking shorter showers, and fixing leaks, you can help save water—especially if you live somewhere with a hot, dry climate!

25% have no access to clean, safe drinking water

In his most viewed video on the Beast Philanthropy page, "We Built Wells in Africa!," MrBeast shares that nearly 2 billion people (about 25% of the planet) do not have access to clean and safe drinking water, so he decided to build 100 wells across Cameroon, Kenya, Somalia, Uganda, and Zimbabwe. In many places in Africa, they say, "Water is Life," and MrBeast recognized that no one should have to live without life's most important resource. Staying in Africa, MrBeast continued his good deeds by delivering solar power to a village ("We Powered a Village in Africa"), building a school in South Africa ("We Built A School"), and partnering with Barefoot No More to deliver shoes to kids who walk miles barefoot just to go to school ("Giving 20,000 Shoes To Kids In Africa"). In Uganda, he found a village (with help from GiveDirectly) where each family received a year's salary to help make life easier.

30,000,000
SQUARE MILES

54
COUNTRIES

2,000
LANGUAGES

! TOTALLY AWESOME FACTS !

AFRICA

1. Africa is HUGE! It is the second-largest continent in the world (after Asia), and it covers nearly 2 million square miles (30 million km²). How big is that? You could take the United States and put it inside of Africa three times, and there would still be room!

2. The continent is made up of 54 countries, including Egypt, Kenya, Nigeria, and Ethiopia. Africa has over 2,000 languages, with Swahili being the most widely spoken.

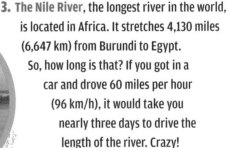

3. **The Nile River**, the longest river in the world, is located in Africa. It stretches 4,130 miles (6,647 km) from Burundi to Egypt. So, how long is that? If you got in a car and drove 60 miles per hour (96 km/h), it would take you nearly three days to drive the length of the river. Crazy!

4. Egypt, which is in northeastern Africa, is home to one of the Seven Wonders of the Ancient World: the **Great Pyramids of Giza**. Built over 4,500 years ago, they are still standing today and can be visited by anyone!

Feeding America

MrBeast made one of his most notable contributions by supporting local food banks in his area. He donated $1 million dollars' worth of meals to families struggling to put food on the table. In his video "Giving $1,000,000 Of Food To People In Need," released on March 27, 2020, MrBeast filled six semitrucks with food like bacon, sausage, ham, and other proteins that are in high demand and delivered them to food banks. Feeding the hungry is yet another of MrBeast's incredible acts of giving back.

Natural Disasters

In addition to improving everyday living conditions all over the planet, MrBeast's generosity extends to those affected by natural disasters. His videos "Rebuilding Homes for Tornado Survivors" and "Helping Hurricane Survivors" have provided hope and stability to families who have been through the unthinkable. Showcasing his dedication to those in crisis, no matter how big or small, or whether they are on foreign or domestic soil, MrBeast's constant actions (in-between his goofy videos and challenges) demonstrate his commitment to using his platform, his influence, and his money to make a positive impact on the lives of others.

JUST REMEMBER . . .

You have the power to change the world. No matter how small your actions may seem—donating a dollar, helping a friend, caring for the environment, supporting a worthy cause you believe in—every act of kindness adds up. There is no small act when it comes to positive change.

CHAPTER

THE BUSINESS OF THE BEAST

THE WILLY WONKA OF
YOUTUBE

A t just 26 years old, MrBeast conquered YouTube by running the most successful channel in the site's history. Most people, after captivating internet audiences and generously giving millions of dollars to those in need, would be satisfied. But MrBeast . . . isn't most people! What did he do next? He took his infectious creativity and bold ideas and expanded his empire beyond the screen.

The Creation of Feastables

MrBeast's first step into expanding his brand was diving headfirst into the world of creating chocolate, with one mission: create the best-tasting, highest-quality candy bars ever! In 2022, he launched Feastables and never looked back. But Feastables isn't your ordinary chocolate bar. With his experience of having Crohn's Disease, he knew that many of the candy bars on the market had way too many ingredients—many of them being unhealthy. Some of those ingredients are so hard to pronounce that you need a chemistry degree to understand them! MrBeast made a pact that he wouldn't sell overly sugary or unhealthy candy bars or snacks to kids. Along with his team, he dedicated his efforts to creating a chocolate bar that had very few ingredients (only four or five). The product launched with three flavors: Original Chocolate, Almond Chocolate, and Quinoa Crunch Chocolate.

A Short History of the
Chocolate Bar

You probably don't think about the history of the chocolate bar when you bite into one. You're just thinking of the sweet taste of chocolate and the big smile it puts on your face! But did you know that the chocolate bar has been around for hundreds of years?!

The first solid chocolate bar was produced in 1847 by a British company called J.S. Fry & Sons (better known as Fry's). It was made possible by a Watt steam engine used to grind cocoa beans, which allowed factory-scale production. As for the first American chocolate bar, that honor goes to Hershey, which released their first bar in 1900 and quickly became known as the "Great American Chocolate Bar." What is your favorite chocolate bar and why?

Feastables was never just about creating the best chocolate bar ever; it was also about creating an experience for MrBeast's fans. To create these experiences, he channeled none other than the most famous fictional chocolatier of all time: Willy Wonka! Like Wonka, MrBeast knows how to make pretty much anything an adventure. Feastables came with a special code that gave fans a chance to win prizes like Teslas, PlayStations, Super73 Electric Bikes, and Beats by Dre headphones. Others got $10,000 for just buying the candy when in the presence of MrBeast. And in some of the packaging, ten lucky Feastable fans received a Golden Ticket (just like Charlie Bucket in *Charlie and the Chocolate Factory*) with an invitation to compete for a massive prize in a real-life Willy Wonka–like MrBeast Chocolate Factory!

⚡ **FAST FACTS** ⚡

Willy Wonka & His Creator

1. The character of Willy Wonka was created by author **Roald Dahl** in his children's book *Charlie and the Chocolate Factory*, released in 1964.

2. Roald Dahl is the author of some of the most beloved children's books of all time with titles such as *Matilda*, *The BFG*, *James and the Giant Peach*, and *The Fantastic Mr. Fox*. He was also a World War II fighter pilot and spy for MI6 (the British counterpart to America's CIA).

3. Willy Wonka has been portrayed on-screen three times. First by Gene Wilder in *Willy Wonka and the Chocolate Factory* (1971), then Johnny Depp in *Charlie and the Chocolate Factory* (2005), and finally **Timothée Chalamet** in *Wonka* (2023).

Thankfully this epic event was documented in his 2022 video "I Built Willy Wonka's Chocolate Factory!" in which ten contestants survived challenge after challenge to win the deed to the factory (worth $500,000). It had giant candy creations, a chocolate river like in the book and movies, and even a special guest judge who crowned the winner—celebrity chef Gordon Ramsay.

BEST SANDWICH EVER

Behind the scenes, MrBeast was on a 14-day fasting challenge, and said if he broke his fast, he would shave his head. Gordon Ramsay made him a breakfast sandwich SO GOOD that he decided to break his fast and lose his hair for it. MrBeast remarked that in the past he's had a $70,000 pizza, $100,000 ice cream, and $10,000 steak, but this sandwich was the best thing he had ever tasted.

Since that video went viral, Feastables has been steadily growing and changing. There are now eight flavors: Milk Chocolate, Peanut Butter, Milk Crunch, Peanut Butter Crunch, Almond, Dark Chocolate, Dark Chocolate Sea Salt, and Cookies & Cream. The brand even expanded to include a fruity twist: Karl's Gummies, a line of gummies inspired by Beast Gang member Karl Jacobs. But MrBeast's sole focus with this brand has been to dethrone chocolate giant Hershey as the best-selling chocolate bar on the market. MrBeast even did a blind taste test with hundreds of strangers who tasted chocolate from Cadbury to Lindt, Feastables was the most preferred. Suffice it to say, Feastables may be around for a long time, especially if MrBeast wants to defeat Hershey.

CREATING A BURGER: BEAST STYLE

Before MrBeast created his own chocolate brand, he decided to do the unthinkable: create a virtual restaurant (which means no dine-in locations) that would deliver hot and tasty burgers right to your door. In December 2020, right in the middle of the global pandemic, people were ordering food from home more than ever. MrBeast saw an opportunity to create something unique that was a way for his fans to interact with his brand. He worked with what he called "ghost kitchens," existing restaurants that could take MrBeast orders and prepare and deliver the food. It started across hundreds of locations, and MrBeast sold 1 million burgers in just three months! Now, MrBeast Burger locations are in several countries around the world and feature burgers designed by MrBeast and some of his Beast Gang.

MRBEAST BURGER

The MrBeast Burger menu is largely inspired by MrBeast's pals. There is the Chandler-Style Burger, named after Chandler Harlow, and Karl's Deluxe, named after Karl Jacobs. There is also the classic Beast Burger, naturally. Other menu items include chicken sandwiches, impossible burgers, grilled cheese sandwiches, chicken tenders, crinkle fries, and cookies.

Something for everyone!

Naturally the launch of this new brand business was chronicled in the video titled "I Opened A Restaurant That Pays You To Eat At It." MrBeast invited fans to a pop-up location in North Carolina where he gave away money, electronics, and even a car. The line for that pop-up was so long (miles long!) that eventually it had to be shut down by police for holding up traffic. Like all his ventures, the brand continues to expand and offers not only burgers but also an experience. Maximizing on the MrBeast fandom is Zaxby's, a fast-casual restaurant that partnered with MrBeast. They offer an exclusive MrBeast Box that includes their famous chicken fingerz, crinkle fries, cheddar bites, Texas toast, double the sauce, a drink, and a Feastables Milk Chocolate bar, all in a collectible box.

WHAT IF YOU COULD design your own burger for MrBeast? What would you put on it? What would you name it? Is it spicy, cheesy, piled high with crazy toppings? Maybe it doesn't have meat. Think about the flavors you love the most and how they can make anyone drool with envy!

NOT TOYING AROUND

I n 2024, MrBeast, in collaboration with Moose Toys, announced his new MrBeast Lab toy line. It includes a variety of interactive toys that are engaging, entertaining, and endlessly collectible. The toys made their debut at San Diego Comic Con, the epicenter for all things pop culture!

DO YOU REMEMBER

the first toy you ever received? How about your favorite toy of all-time? Why is it your favorite?

The MrBeast Lab collection includes a variety of interactive toys, including:

- **Swarms:** Over 100 unique micro-collectibles that are revealed through a lab experiment
- **Mutators:** Figures that you open with a unique open-boxing experience, including a fingerprint scanner
- Vinyl figures and collector figures

In addition to his toys, MrBeast has a robust line of merchandise of hats, hoodies, basketballs, footballs, notebooks, and more, so the whole world knows you're a part of the Beast Gang.

BEAST GAMES

 **e's been buried alive,** survived a deserted island, and lived inside a house made entirely of ice, but MrBeast's biggest challenge came when he decided to take a break from YouTube to complete perhaps his greatest achievement: a TV show. MrBeast never wanted his videos to look overproduced or like anything that had existed before. But a TV show opened doors to conquer a new global audience. In true MrBeast fashion, instead of taking small steps, he took one giant leap to create the craziest, most supercharged TV show ever, with crazy challenges, mind-blowing stunts, and a big cash prize. He said he wanted to make the greatest show possible to prove that YouTubers and creators can succeed on other platforms, and thus, *Beast Games* was born.

⚡ FAST FACTS ⚡
Reality TV Competitions

1. The first reality TV show (according to Guinness World Records) is *Candid Camera*, which premiered in 1948 and was a prank show involving practical jokes on unsuspecting members of the public.

2. *Survivor,* which premiered on CBS in 2000, is the reality competition show with the most seasons: 48 and still going. Talk about surviving cancellation!

3. Some music stars got their start or were found on reality TV competition shows: *American Idol* (Kelly Clarkson, Jennifer Hudson, Carrie Underwood), *Star Search* (Usher, Britney Spears, Christina Aguilera, Justin Timberlake, Beyoncé), *The X Factor UK* (One Direction, Leona Lewis, Little Mix).

One filming location for *Beast Games* was **Allegiant Stadium**, a 10-level domed stadium in Las Vegas, Nevada. Thanks to Mark Davis, the owner of the Raiders, the professional football team that plays there, the stadium is nicknamed "Death Star" because of its sleek, black facade that resembles the ominous moon-sized space station of Darth Vader and the Empire. Many fans of the Raiders aren't fond of the name, as the *Death Star* from the *Star Wars* films (despite its size and power) was destroyed twice. The stadium has also been affectionately nicknamed "Roomba" for its resemblance to the robotic vacuum from an overhead view.

What is *Beast Games*? A competition show featuring 1,000 contestants who are competing for a massive cash prize—the show tests the participants' endurance, wits, and willpower. This time, however, MrBeast didn't just give away $10,000 here or $500,000 there. The grand prize was $5 million, making it the largest cash prize in the history of TV and streaming!

PRIOR TO BEAST GAMES,

the largest competition prize ever awarded was $4.65 million to Mai Whelan, an immigration adjudicator who beat out 400 contestants on *Squid Game: The Challenge* on Netflix. Whelan ended up winning the massive grand prize during a round of **rock paper scissors**.

A BEAST OF A
LEGACY

He may not have thought it was possible when he first started making videos at 11 years old, but MrBeast will undoubtedly leave a massive asteroid-size mark on the world of content creation. But luckily for MrBeast (and fans of his videos and giveaways), his legacy is still in the making. After all, he's still young! MrBeast hit his first 100 million subscribers just shy of his 25th birthday. That's pretty crazy! Sure, he had been working his butt off and making videos for almost 15 years before that happened, but to become successful, that young, is not only a rarity, but super impressive!

The Young Achievers

CLUB

There's no rule in the book of life that you have to become successful by a certain age. Some people hit it big at a young age, others don't become famous until they turn 50, and many never become famous at all. And you know what? All these options are okay! But it's certainly fun to learn about those famous figures who seemed to accomplish the impossible. Here's a collection of young achievers who solidified their names in the history books before age 30.

Alexander the Great

By age 30, Alexander created one of the largest empires in history from Macedonia to Egypt and from Greece to part of India. He's considered one of the greatest military commanders of all time and earned the nickname "the Great" because he never lost a battle.

Mary Shelley

Author Mary Shelley created one of history's most beloved monsters when she published her book, *Frankenstein*, in 1818 at age 20. Initially, was published anonymously, but over 200 years later, everyone knows Shelley's name and her impact.

Mark Zuckerberg

He may not be Bill Gates (who cofounded Microsoft by age 20 and by 31 became the world's youngest billionaire), but Mark Zuckerberg certainly made his own mark cofounding Facebook at age 23. Since then, he's played a significant role in the world's digital landscape.

Mozart

Composer Wolfgang Amadeus Mozart composed his first music at age 5, his first symphony at 8, and his first opera at age 12! Known for works like Requiem, The Magic Flute, and The Marriage of Figaro, Mozart composed over 600 works before his death at age 35.

Serena Williams

Considered by many to be the GOAT of women's tennis and arguably the GOAT of all tennis, Serena, by age 20, had won four Grand Slam singles titles (the French Open, Wimbledon, US Open, the Australian Open), which became known as a "Serena Slam."

MrBeast has not only redefined what it means to be a YouTuber, but also what it means to be a person with incredible influence with the way he approaches philanthropy and business. Every year, his videos get bigger, the prizes get bigger, and as evident by his campaigns to plant trees and clean up the seas, he's clearly set his sights on making a difference not just in North Carolina, but globally. In 2024, he even remarked on social media that he would gladly run for president of the United States, but he needs to wait until he's old enough as the required age to run for president is 35 years old.

WOULD YOU VOTE

for MrBeast for president? If you could vote for anyone to be president, regardless of age or what job they had, who would be the best person for the job? A parent, a teacher, a celebrity, an athlete? Who has your vote?

Whatever the future holds for MrBeast, this is certain: he will continue to inspire millions with his relentless drive, generosity, and passion for what he does. To inspire you on your journey toward building a legacy and changing the world, remember these words from MrBeast himself:

"You're crazy until you're successful.
Then you are a genius."

WOULD YOU RATHER:
BEAST-STYLE

Have you ever dreamed about what it would be like to live in MrBeast's world of epic challenges and mind-blowing stunts? Or maybe you're waiting for the day that you get to be a contestant or the subject in one of his videos. This book may not have magical powers to make all that a reality, but it can give you inspiration to make similar, tough (and sometimes hilarious) choices.

It's time to dive into a collection of "Would You Rather?" questions to debate with your friends. You will be given two scenarios, from serious to silly, strange to downright crazy, and some inspired by MrBeast's videos. All you have to do is think about which scenario sounds better and explain why you chose it! Buckle up, use your imagination, and let these questions make you think, laugh, and dream big—just like MrBeast!

WOULD YOU RATHER . . .

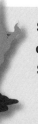

Survive a zombie apocalypse with the members of BTS (inside a Dick's Sporting Goods) or join Ed Sheeren, the Jonas Brothers, and Selena Gomez at an all-night concert at your school?

Only eat Feastables chocolate for the rest of your life or be paid $1 million, but you can never eat chocolate again?

Be trained in gymnastics by Livvy Dunne or learn how to shoot a three-point shot by Caitlin Clark?

Play hockey on a moving glacier in Antarctica or play basketball next to a volcano?

Barbecue with LeBron James on a private yacht or go skiing with Dwayne "The Rock" Johnson and drink the world's most expensive hot chocolate?

Live in a grocery store for 30 days for $100,000 or live without electronics for 30 days for $500,000?

Have a rewind button or a pause button for your life?

Spend a night in a haunted house with 500 nonvenomous spiders or fly from Los Angeles to New York in a plane with 100 snakes?

Compete in a giant food fight featuring all your favorite foods or participate in a paintball battle in a working amusement park with free rides?

Get a year's supply of your favorite food or go on an all-expenses-paid trip anywhere in the world?

BEST OF THE
BEAST

With over 1,000 videos across all his channels (and getting very close to 100 billion views total), MrBeast has created more content than you could binge in a single weekend. Come to think of it, maybe that could be your very first MrBeast-style YouTube video challenge:

"I WATCHED ALL OF MRBEAST'S VIDEOS IN ONE SITTING!"

He's done outrageous challenges, shown heartwarming acts of kindness, awarded massive giveaways, and expressed no signs of stopping! MrBeast's videos have something for everyone. But with so many videos to choose from, where do you start? Well, this section has you covered, compiling 10 Top 5 lists that are perfect for creating your own ultimate MrBeast playlist. Plus, for all you superfans who watch every video the second it drops, these will be great icebreakers to inspire debate among your friends about your favorite moments.

Showdowns

"100 Assassins Vs 10 Real Cops!"

"100 Boys Vs 100 Girls For $500,000"

"100 Kids Vs 100 Adults For $500,000"

"50 YouTubers Fight For $1,000,000"

"Ages 1 - 100 Fight For $500,000"

Competition

"Last To Leave the Circle Wins $500,000"

"Every Country On Earth Fights For $250,000!"

"World's Deadliest Obstacle Course!"

"Extreme $100,000 Game of Tag!"

"$456,000 *Squid Game* in Real Life!"

Philanthropy Projects

"I Built 100 Wells In Africa"

"I Built 100 Houses And Gave Them Away!"

"I Helped 2,000 People Walk Again"

"1,000 Blind People See For The First Time"

"1,000 Deaf People Hear For The First Time"

Crazy Destructions

"I Bought The World's Largest Firework ($600,000)"

"Protect $500,000 Keep It!"

"Train Vs Giant Pit"

"Protect The Lamborghini, Keep It!"

"Lamborghini Vs World's Largest Shredder"

MrBeast Classics

"Reading The Entire *Bee Movie* Script But Everytime They Say 'Bee' I Repeat All the Previous Bees"

"Watching Dance Till You're Dead For 10 Hours"

"Giving My Mom $100,000 (Proudest Day Of My Life)"

"Giving A Random Homeless Man $10,000"

"I Counted To 100,000!"

Behind the
BULL

Lamborghini was founded in Italy in 1963 by Ferruccio Lamborghini to compete with Ferrari in producing high-performance sports cars. While Ferrari's famous logo features a prancing horse, the Lamborghini logo is a buff bull. If you are looking into buying your first Lambo (and who isn't?), their top model is the **Lamborghini Revuelto**. The 2024 model boasts a 6.5-liter V12 engine paired with three electric motors, producing 1,001 horsepower and 535 pound-feet of torque. It has a top speed of 217 miles per hour (436 km/h) and accelerates from 0 to 60 miles per hour (97 km/h) in just 2.5 seconds. You can have all that for the low, low price of $608,000!

Most Expensive Comparisons

"$1 Vs $250,000,000 Private Island!"

"$1 Vs $100,000,000 Car!"

"$1 Vs $1,000,000 Yacht!"

"$1 Vs $1,000,000 Hotel Room!"

"$1 Vs $500,000 Plane Ticket!"

Creative Builds

"I Built A Mansion Using Only Cardboard Boxes"

"I Built Willy Wonka's Chocolate Factory!"

"I Built A Working Car Using Only LEGOS"

"I Built The World's Largest Lego Tower"

"I Built 100 Houses And Gave Them Away!"

I Spent

"I Spent 24 Hours Straight In Slime"

"I Spent 24 Hours Straight At Area 51"

"I Spent 24 Hours Straight In Prison"

"I Spent 7 Days In Solitary Confinement"

"I Spent 7 Days Buried Alive"

I Survived

"I Survived 50 Hours In A Maximum Security Prison"

"I Survived A Plane Crash"

"I Survived 50 Hours In Antarctica"

"I Survived 7 Days In An Abandoned City"

"I Survived 24 Hours Straight In Ice"

WHICH OF THE

above survival challenges do you think you'd have the best shot at winning?

Shorts

"I Tipped A Pizza Delivery Driver A Car"

"Guess The Gift, Keep It"

"Katana Vs Bullet"

"Would You Fly To Paris For A Baguette?"

"Giving iPhones Instead Of Candy on Halloween"

FEASTABLE
FACTS

With billions of views across all his platforms, MrBeast is the most viewed YouTuber in the galaxy, but how much do you actually know about him behind-the-scenes? You know he loves challenges. You know he loves giving away huge piles of cash. And you know he loves helping out those in need. But what about the man behind the brand? Here are 15 Feastable facts about the man behind the empire!

New Heights

It might be hard to see in his videos, but MrBeast is very tall. In fact, he's one of the tallest YouTubers around. MrBeast tweeted in 2023 that he was measured at 6 feet, 5 inches and thinks he's still growing.

RECORD-BREAKERS

The Tallest Person in History: Robert Pershing Wadlow, born in Alton, Illinois, in 1918, still holds the record as the World's Tallest Person at an incredible 8 feet, 11 inches. Basically, 9 feet tall! Currently, the World's Tallest Person is Sultan Kosen, a Turkish farmer, who stands at 8 feet, 2.82 inches.

Here is a list of the tallest players in history for each of the big four leagues:
NBA: **Manute Bol and Gheorghe Muresan – 7 feet, 7 inches**
NFL: **Richard Sligh – 7 feet**
NHL: **Zdeno Chára – 6 feet, 9 inches**
MLB: **Jon Rauch, Sean Hjelle – 6 feet, 11 inches**

6'5"

Astrological Sign

Taurus

A Future in Acting?

MrBeast has a small cameo in
Kung Fu Panda 4 as Panda Pig
and a cameo in *Teenage Mutant
Ninja Turtles: Mutant Mayhem*
as Times Square Guy.

Pets

MrBeast shares a cat named Satan with
his fiancée, South African YouTuber,
author, and Twitch streamer,
Thea Booysen.

Biggest Fear

Aviophobia or aerophobia, aka the fear of flying. Being MrBeast
means you have to fly all over the world, so how does
MrBeast conquer his fear on a repeated basis? He recites
statistics about how safe flying is (1 in 13 million chance of
death), and during takeoff, he closes his eyes and cranks up
music, so he doesn't realize he's already in the air.

Never Watched

ANIME?

"Anime" is the shortened form of the Japanese word *animēshon*, which simply translates to "animation." Here are three anime movies worth checking out. Creators prefer if you watch anime in its native Japanese with subtitles, but if you want to ease your way in, try the dubbed versions.

1. *Spirited Away*: A 10-year-old girl named Chihiro stumbles into a world of spirits and gods and must navigate her way through in order to save her parents and find her way back home.

2. *My Hero Academia*: In a world where almost everyone has superpowers, a determined boy named Izuku, who was born without powers, inherits the abilities of the world's greatest superhero and enrolls in a hero academy.

3. *Pokémon*: A young trainer named Ash travels the world with his friends and his Pokémon (creatures with magical powers) while fending off various challenges and rivals on his journey to becoming a Pokémon Master.

MrBeast Recommends

A heated toilet seat—he says it will change your life.

Loving Anime

When he has downtime (which is almost never), MrBeast enjoys watching anime with titles like *Attack on Titan*, *Death Note*, and *Naruto* being some of his favorites.

Hardest Challenge

MrBeast admitted that his video "I Spent 7 Days Buried Alive" was his hardest challenge, and despite having a photo of Nolan's mom to keep him company, it didn't help the back pain.

Favorite YouTube Channels

MrBeast says that when he watches YouTube he likes to learn. His favorite channels are Wendover Productions, Polymatter, Mark Rober, Veratasium, and Marques Brownlee, to name a few.

Good Morning

The first app MrBeast opens in the morning is Twitter/X. He also has a handshake deal with X owner Elon Musk that if Musk dies, MrBeast gets to take it over.

WE KNOW YOU

love MrBeast, but what are some of your other favorite YouTube channels?

Favorite Food

His mom's chicken teriyaki.

Favorite Board Game

Catan (formerly known as The Settlers of Catan).

THE FEATS OF THE
BEAST

MrBeast is living proof that if you set your mind to something, anything is possible! At just 27 years old (not even 30 yet!), MrBeast has racked up an incredible list of awards, accolades, and jaw-dropping feats that some people spend an entire life chasing. MrBeast spends so much time helping others that he probably doesn't realize everything he's accomplished. Why? Because the list is so long! Here are just a few (of many) highlights that MrBeast has achieved both on and off YouTube, including his personal list of accomplishments that reside on his YouTube channel in his own words.

ACCOMPLISHMENTS

MrBeast has a long-running, constantly updated list of achievements posted on his MrBeast YouTube channel. Here are some highlights, among many!

- **Removed 30,000,000 pounds (14 million kg) of trash from the ocean**

- **Helped 2,000 people walk again**

- **Helped 1,000 blind people see**

- **Helped 1,000 deaf people hear**

- Built wells in Africa

- Built and gave away 100 houses

- Gave millions to charity

- Started my own snack company Feastables

- Started my own software company Viewstats

- Created the largest competition show with 1000 people (*Beast Games*)

STREAMY AWARDS

(awards given for the best online video and best content creators)

- **Breakout Creator**
- **4x Creator of the Year**
- **Live Special**
- **2x Social Good Creator**
- **Social Good: Nonprofit or NGO**
- **Brand Engagement**
- **Collaboration**

Forbes

OTHER AWARDS + ACCOLADES

TIME

- *Forbes* highest-earning YouTube creator
- *Forbes* 30 Under 30
- 3x Nickelodeon Kids' Choice Award (Favorite Male Creator)
- Shorty Award YouTuber of the Year
- *Time* 100 most influential people (2023)
- Over 300 million subscribers on YouTube

GUINNESS WORLD RECORDS

- Highest-earning YouTube contributor
- Largest vegetarian burger
- Most subscribers for an individual male on YouTube
- First person to reach 1 million followers on Threads
- Most subscribers on YouTube
- Most subscribers gained in a week
- Most Cameras Used in a Single Production (*Beast Games*)

113

THE ULTIMATE
MRBEAST QUIZ

You've gotten all the way to the end of this book. What does that mean? Well, you should know everything there is to know about MrBeast! And guess what? We're going to test it. Below are 10 questions about MrBeast using information that you've already learned while flipping through these pages. See how well you score and then test your friends and family!

1

MrBeast practically put Greenville, North Carolina, on the map with construction of his mega–YouTube studios located all around the area. But let's see if you remember where he came from. What NFL team would Jimmy be a fan of based on the city where he was born?

A. Denver Broncos (Denver, Colorado)

B. Kansas City Chiefs (Wichita, Kansas)

C. Tennessee Titans (Nashville, Tennessee)

D. Arizona Cardinals (Glendale, Arizona)

The Big Game

The Super Bowl is the NFL's crown-jewel spectacle capturing hearts and raising the blood pressure of millions of fans around the world. The **first Super Bowl** took place on January 15, 1967, and pitted the Green Bay Packers against the Kansas City Chiefs. This was the beginning of one of the biggest annual sporting events in the world. Today, the Super Bowl is watched by millions of people, not just for the game, but for the star-studded halftime show and iconic commercials. Speaking of commercials, in 1967, a 30-second advertisement would cost you $42,500 to purchase. Fast-forward to 2025, and you'd have to pay $8 million. For 30 seconds!

Wisconsin Native

Donald A. Gorske holds the Guinness world record for the most **Big Macs** ever eaten. He's eaten at least one Big Mac every single day since 1972 and is currently at 34,000 Big Macs eaten and is still going! The first time he had the iconic sandwich was in 1972 when he ate three Big Macs, fries and a Coke all for $1.87! Did you know that one McDonald's Big Mac has 590 calories, 25g of protein, 46g of carbs, and 34g of total fat?

2 Which sport did MrBeast play before discovering YouTube?

    A. Golf

    B. Soccer

    C. Wrestling

    D. Baseball

3 Sorry if this makes you hungry, but what is the name of MrBeast's fast-food restaurant chain that he opened in 2020 and features menu items inspired by him and his Beast Gang?

    A. MrBeast Burger

    B. Epic Feast

    C. MegaBeast Grill

    D. Beastly Burgers & Fries

Who is NOT a member of the Beast Gang?

    A. Chandler

    B. Kal Pal

    C. Tareq

    D. Karl

 What video did MrBeast release in 2017 that helped him go viral for the first time (getting tens of thousands of views) and was a turning point in his career?

    A. "I Recited Every Word In The Phone Book!"

    B. "I Stared At A Poster Of Bugs Bunny For 2 Hours!"

    C. "I Counted To 100,000!"

    D. "I Slept For 3 Days Straight!"

  go viral with a video, what kind of personal challenge do you think you could handle to do it? What kind of challenge would you want to do?

 You've probably seen MrBeast's logo too many times to count. But do you know what kind of Beast is pictured on the logo? (At least when he started.)

    A. Lion

    B. Tiger

    C. Jaguar

    D. Leopard

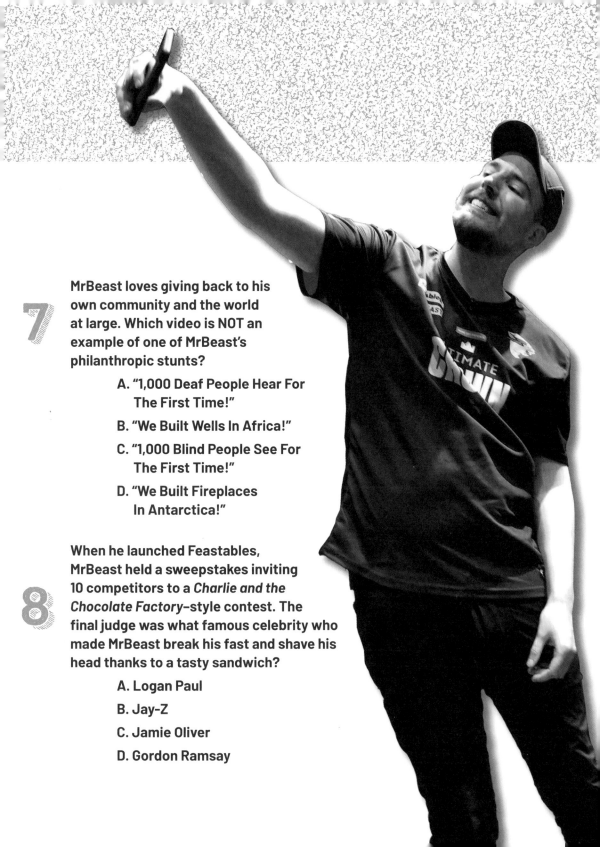

7

MrBeast loves giving back to his own community and the world at large. Which video is NOT an example of one of MrBeast's philanthropic stunts?

    A. "1,000 Deaf People Hear For The First Time!"

    B. "We Built Wells In Africa!"

    C. "1,000 Blind People See For The First Time!"

    D. "We Built Fireplaces In Antarctica!"

8

When he launched Feastables, MrBeast held a sweepstakes inviting 10 competitors to a *Charlie and the Chocolate Factory*–style contest. The final judge was what famous celebrity who made MrBeast break his fast and shave his head thanks to a tasty sandwich?

    A. Logan Paul

    B. Jay-Z

    C. Jamie Oliver

    D. Gordon Ramsay

What Is
NASA?

NASA is short for the National Aeronautics and Space Administration, and, for lack of a better description, it's like the coolest science club ever. NASA is part of the US government and is known for sending astronauts to space, discovering mind-blowing things about our universe, and inventing new technologies that impact our daily lives. Here are five influential people from NASA's history that you should know about!

Neil Armstrong

In 1969 (during the Apollo 11 mission), Ohio native and Purdue University graduate Neil Armstrong became the first human to walk on the moon. While on the extraterrestrial surface, Armstrong famously said the words, "One small step for man, one giant leap for mankind."

Katherine Johnson

Often referred to as the "Woman of the 20th Century," Katherine Johnson was a brilliant mathematician whose calculations were crucial to the success of the first US space mission to orbit the Earth.

Sally Ride

After Soviet cosmonaut (astronaut) Valentina Tereshkova became the first woman in space, Sally Ride became the first American woman in space. While traveling aboard the space shuttle *Challenger* in 1983, Ride inspired future generations of women in STEM (science, technology, engineering, and mathematics) fields.

Mae Jemison

Engineer, physician, and NASA astronaut, Mae Jemison is the first African American woman to travel into space during her time aboard the space shuttle *Endeavour* in 1992.

9 The #TeamSeas campaign (which, as of 2024, has removed over 34 million pounds, or 15 million kg, of trash from beaches, rivers, and oceans) was a partnership with which friend of MrBeast? Hint: He is a fellow YouTuber and former NASA engineer.

    A. Simone Giertz

    B. Nick Echols

    C. Mark Rober

    D. Hank Green

 **IF YOU WERE AN** astronaut, what planet would be first on your list to explore?

10 What famous YouTuber did MrBeast initially look up to; make videos about; and ultimately pass in popularity, views, and subscribers when he hit it big?

    A. PewDiePie

    B. Doofus88

    C. Olive0rTwi5T

    D. Zenmaster6000

BE LIKE THE BEAST:
THE AT-HOME CHALLENGE

Hey future YouTube legends! You probably thought this book was over, but wait, there's one more surprise! As you begin your journey toward becoming the next MrBeast, make sure you have a cool channel name ready to go! It's time to take part in your own set of challenges just like the man himself. Don't worry; there will be no live snakes or blowing up sports cars. We've put together 10 different challenges with 3 different levels of difficulty, perfect for all ages and experience levels. You can choose just one level, or if you want to Beast it and be super ambitious, take on all three.

It's time to make amazing memories, learn new skills, help your fellow Earth-dwelling mammals, and most of all, have fun! Good luck!

READY . . . SET . . . GO . . .

The Giveaway Challenge

Level 1: Pay a stranger a compliment.

Level 2: Donate a toy or piece of clothing to a shelter or Goodwill/Salvation Army.

Level 3: Save up $20 from chores, buy a gift card, and give it to a stranger.

The Dictionary Challenge

Level 1: Learn a new word. Spell it. Say it correctly. Then secretly use it in a conversation.

Level 2: Learn a new word and write a one-page story inspired by the word.

Level 3: Find 10 extremely challenging words. Quiz your parents on their definitions at the dinner table.

The Creative Build Challenge

Level 1: Using LEGO blocks, build something that's half your size.

Level 2: Using cardboard boxes, build a fort in your room.

Level 3: Using whatever you have available, build an obstacle course in your yard or at a park. Get your friends to try it out.

The 1-Week Challenge

Level 1: Do not use the words "can't," "stupid," or "hate" for one week.

Level 2: Do not eat any candy or food with added sugar for one week.

Level 3: Do not (pick 1) watch TV, play video games, use a computer, or use a tablet for one week.

The Chore Challenge

Level 1: Help clean the dishes.

Level 2: Help mow the lawn or shovel snow or take out the garbage.

Level 3: Help your parents with one of their chores for three days in a row.

The Positive Interaction Challenge

Level 1: Choose one of your favorite books (that you don't need anymore) and gift it to someone.

Level 2: Pick three people who impact your life positively and write them a thank-you note.

Level 3: Find a senior citizen and ask them five questions about their life.

The Group Challenge (at least three people required)

Level 1: Get a group together. Everyone stands on one leg. Last person standing wins.

Level 2: Get a group together. Put on a music playlist. Start dancing. Last person dancing wins.

Level 3: Get a group together. Everyone makes 10 water balloons or 10 snowballs. Set a timer for 10 minutes. The person who is the driest wins.

The Solo Challenge

Level 1: Read one book (at least 100 pages) in one sitting. Don't stop until you're done.

Level 2: Watch one movie trilogy in one day. Bathroom breaks allowed!

Level 3: Go a whole day without speaking. Be creative!

The Food Challenge

Level 1: Try one piece of a food you've never had before.

Level 2: Try one beverage that you've never had before.

Level 3: Try one meal from a style of cuisine you've never had before.

The Learning Challenge

Level 1: Pick a letter from the alphabet and learn about a historical figure with a first or last name starting with that letter.

Level 2: Ask a parent, guardian, teacher, or friend about one of their favorite skills and have them teach it to you.

Level 3: Pick a musical instrument, hobby, choreographed dance, art project, or language and spend one month learning it. Practice every day. After one month, see how you like it. Worst case scenario, you taught yourself something new! Always be learning!

PHOTO CREDITS

ACKNOWLEDGMENTS

In the middle of writing this book, I was whisked away to Ireland to appear on season two of *The Floor*, where I pretended to know everything about world currencies and ultimately walked away with zero currencies of any kind (thanks, migraines). But I did win something even better—99 new lifelong friends, a.k.a. my forever floormily. "Feet!"

Thanks to Rob Lowe for letting me call you Dean Youngblood, complimenting my subterfuge, and literally dapping me up in front of millions of people. To all the truly amazing crew behind the scenes—your hard work did not go unnoticed.

Thanks to my wife, Colleen, my family, and my friends for all their love and support. To my agent, Justin Brouckaert of Aevitas Creative Management, for your guidance. To Nicole James, for letting me kick off this series and being the best editor around! To the design team—you never disappoint.

And to MrBeast—after watching nearly every video you've ever made and sampling all your Feastables flavors, my mind, body, and soul are ready to be the star of your next video. I hope you had a 100% retention rate reading my tribute to your life. My DMs are open.

ABOUT THE AUTHOR

NEAL E. FISCHER is a former band geek, theater nerd, and prom king, and he was raised on movies totally inappropriate for a five-year-old. (Turned out just fine!) He loves all things pop culture and is known to dominate your favorite trivia night. He was even a contestant on season two of the Rob Lowe-hosted game show, *The Floor*. Neal is a former children's theater director and the author of *The Totally Awesome World of Steph Curry* and *The Totally Awesome World of Cristiano Ronaldo*, among many other pop culture titles on a variety of subjects. He wishes he could grow facial hair and once offered Tom Cruise dinner. Neal lives in Chicago with his wife, Colleen, a theater director and special education instructor.

First published in 2025 by becker&mayer!kids, an imprint of The Quarto Group, 142 West 36th Street, 4th Floor, New York, NY 10018, USA (212) 779-4972 • www.Quarto.com

becker&mayer!kids titles are also available at discount for retail, wholesale, promotional, and bulk purchase. For details, contact the Special Sales Manager by email at specialsales@quarto.com or by mail at The Quarto Group, Attn: Special Sales Manager, 100 Cummings Center Suite 265D, Beverly, MA 01915 USA.

10 9 8 7 6 5 4 3 2 1

ISBN: 978-0-7603-9543-1

Digital edition published in 2025
eISBN: 978-0-7603-9544-8

Library of Congress Control Number: 2024947078

Group Publisher: Rage Kindelsperger
Creative Director: Laura Drew
Managing Editor: Cara Donaldson
Editor: Nicole James
Text: Neal E. Fischer
Cover Illustration: Jamie Coe
Cover Design: Scott Richardson
Interior Design: Brad Norr Design

Printed in China

LEXILE®

Lexile® 1110L